D1389150

PRACTICAL HANDBOOKS FOR COLLECTORS

*

BRITISH COMMONWEALTH COINAGE

COINS

OLD CLOCKS

OLD COPPER AND BRASS

COTTAGE AND FARMHOUSE FURNITURE

OLD GLASS

OLD PRINTS

OLD SHEFFIELD PLATE

OLD SILVER

*

PRACTICAL HANDBOOKS FOR COLLECTORS

COINS

By the same author

BRITISH COMMONWEALTH COINAGE

THE CROWN PIECES OF GREAT BRITAIN AND THE BRITISH COMMONWEALTH

EARLY AEROPLANES

AEROPLANES OF WORLD WAR I

*

BEGINNER'S GUIDE TO COIN COLLECTING

Silver Pound Piece of Charles I, struck at Shrewsbury
(*See p. 80, note 53*)

COINS

By

HOWARD W. A. LINECAR

THIRD EDITION

LONDON · ERNEST BENN LIMITED

First published 1955 by Ernest Benn Limited
Bouverie House · Fleet Street · London · EC4
New and enlarged edition 1962
Third edition 1967

Printed in Great Britain

TO

MY WIFE

IN GRATITUDE FOR HER HELP

Preface to the Third Edition

It is indeed a great pleasure to know that this book has been so well received that a third edition has been asked for. Since it was first published in 1955 coin and medal collecting has steadily increased as more people have found something of the great interests that lie behind the apparently formidable word, numismatics. Not only are there more collectors and students of the subject, but more books are being written dealing with every aspect of numismatics, to help not only the beginner but the more advanced. Such a great project as the *Sylloge of Coins of the British Isles,* commenced in 1958, is now well under way, with nine volumes published and more to come. New books have appeared dealing with the British Sovereign, with Greek and Roman coins: Dr. Davenport's three important volumes dealing with the crown-size coins of Europe have been reprinted and brought up to date. A modest start has been made with that almost impossible work, a catalogue of the coins of the world. To the *Catalog of Modern World Coins* (covering from about 1850 to date) there has recently been added the book *Coins of the World, 1750–1850.* Handy pocket guides on a large number of series of coins have continued to multiply, and still the flow of useful works at all levels of the science increases.

That there is room for all these books: that they are being written, sold and studied is the most solid indication possible of the great increase in interest. Not only are they sold to individual collectors and students but so great has the demand become that Public Libraries, Reference Libraries and the libraries of colleges, schools and museums have been adding to their shelves many volumes dealing with coins and medals and allied subjects. Such institutions only spend their hard-won book grants on such volumes because they have been asked for by their students and their public.

Such a demand has arisen in part from the fact that increasing leisure and a higher standard of living have produced more people who would use some of their leisure on something worth while. In part it has arisen from the fact that more people realise that a properly built coin or medal collection, as well as interesting and instructing its owner, giving him many hours of pleasure, is also a sound investment. It matters not how humble the subject may be, if the collection has been built with care and judgment its value will increase, since it is an entity and time, thought and money have been put into its formation.

To give some guidance on how this subject of coin collecting and investment should be undertaken books such as this volume have been written. It is heartening to know that they are of some help and that they are appreciated.

1967 H. LINECAR

Preface to the Second Edition

It was with a feeling of genuine pleasure that I accepted the invitation of my publisher to prepare a second edition of *Coins*. Genuine pleasure because it was obvious that, a very considerable first edition having been exhausted, there was still a demand for more. So, more there shall be.

Since *Coins* was first published neither history nor numismatics has been idle. New issues of coins have continued, new knowledge has been recorded. Some of the former are beyond the scope of these pages. Much of the latter is too highly specialised for a general work of this nature. Where appropriate, however, some reference has been made. As an example of the first, large numbers of sovereigns have been struck once more by the Royal Mint. Of the latter: the long-awaited catalogue of the copper, tin and bronze coins of Britain has been published.

Further chapters have been added. One gives something of more interest to the collector of British Commonwealth coinages. Another says something about coins and collectors in Canada and the United States. The bibliography has been revised and greatly extended and the index has been recompiled.

As I have tried to indicate, once afloat on the numismatic sea, one can set one's course in that direction which appears the most promising. It is in the hope of indicating a few of the possible courses that this second edition, careened and somewhat refitted, is launched.

LONDON 1962 H. L.

Preface to the First Edition

SINCE there already exists a legion of books on every aspect of coins – their history and development, their significance in history and their acquisition by collectors, this book only tries to introduce a large subject to those who know little or nothing of it. It hopes to stimulate an interest in that most worthy study, the science of numismatics. It makes no pretence at being a work of reference apart from its appendices, which may be some help to those starting to collect.

Till recent years beginners in the study of coins have been but meagrely catered for. Many of the erudite works on the subject have a forbidding aspect. It is in the hope that it may have some popular appeal that this book has been written. The well-known series to which it belongs is its sufficient advertisement. In spite of all that modern entertainment can offer there are more serious readers today than ever before, and this book may introduce to them a new line of thought on a subject hitherto outside their usual sphere.

I should like to record my thanks to those who have kindly helped in the preparation. In particular to the late Charles Seltman, Litt. D., the late Raymond Carlyon-Britton, and Arthur Linecar, who looked over the proofs and made many valuable suggestions. Also to the Keeper of Coins and Medals in the British Museum for permission to illustrate coins from the National Collection.

LONDON 1955 H. L.

Contents

Illustrations

CHAPTER ONE

The Evolution of Coinage

AT THE present time a coin has little value. It is simply a promise to pay in goods, to be selected by the purchaser. In the early dawn of civilisation there was no money as we know it now. Goods were exchanged for other goods, and from this there developed a system of values. A certain commodity, for example an ox, was rated as being worth a certain amount of food or other essential goods. This system had obvious disadvantages. Any animate medium of exchange might die, thus rendering the owner that much the poorer. Its exchange value might be disputed between the contracting parties. Any such system of exchange and barter could only function in a very limited way in a country or community run on the very simplest form of economy. In the search for essentials, such as food, the purchaser might be forced by circumstance to offer in exchange that which he could ill afford. Conversely, in disposing of a surplus of one commodity he might be obliged to receive that for which he had no great immediate need.

Obviously some form of intermediary of a fixed value was required. Between the selling of an ox and the buying of food, those concerned needed some item of the same value as the ox and the food. This item had to be easily portable, and had to be accepted on all sides and by all people as of a definite value. To fill this gap coins were gradually evolved. They were, doubtless, one of the first objects of a purely functional design.

No one man invented coins. They were evolved by a gradual process. At first they were little better than pieces of metal stamped in some way which would be recognisable by all as imparting to them the status of a fixed medium of exchange. The evolution of coins and the development of their design follows in direct relationship to the growth in size and complexity of any civilisation.

A relatively small civilisation, one which did not tend to expand greatly beyond its own natural boundaries, was that of

Ancient Egypt. It contrived to carry on its economic life, until the Ptolemaic period of its history, without the use of coins as we understand them.

Ancient Greece, consisting in the main of a number of small city states, found the need for coins more acute. Relationship between the various states and with an expanding world had to be maintained. Since the Greeks had a great veneration for beauty in all its forms, it followed that Greek coins were also things of beauty. This beauty has, in the numismatic world, never been surpassed.

The Ancient Romans ruled an expanding Empire. It was acquired mainly by conquest and held together by armed might. The countries which it acquired in its expansion were often less civilised than itself. It was deemed necessary to introduce into each country acquired the Roman system. This system brought with it Roman Law and Roman money. The effects of the Roman legal and monetary systems are still largely the basis on which their modern equivalents are founded.

As the Roman Empire grew its outposts moved farther away from the centre of the Empire, the City of Rome. The outposts were maintained and the Empire held together by armies and an excellent system of direct road communications. The armies had to be paid, and wherever they were garrisoned Roman coins may be found. If they were not so readily accepted by the less civilised inhabitants whose country had been annexed, then the inhabitants had to be educated to the system. After the recall of the Legions (*circa* 395), Roman influence remained sufficiently strong to cause the garrisoned countries to imitate Roman methods, even Roman coins. It remained strong enough to survive in part the Dark Ages.

Though within their known world the Romans travelled far, by modern standards they were not great travellers. The extent of their maritime explorations seems to have been the British Isles and a certain amount of coasting round Africa. In the main, only the soldiers and those connected with the armies and with government travelled any distance. Popular mass travel was unknown. No doubt some of the more adventurous sailed from the landlocked Mediterranean into the uncharted waters of the Atlantic, but their maritime powers were limited by the development of their vessels, propelled by sail and oar. But wherever their influence extended their coins may be found, and these coins carried numismatic development a stage farther. Whereas Greek coins were, in large measure, used to display the Greek gods, Greek local environment and the Greek way of life, Roman coins gradually evolved a more political significance. Heads of Emperors began to appear with quasi-political or political legends and other local propaganda. Both the Greek and Roman models have been faithfully followed by later civilisations. Local legendary characters, rulers, habitations, emblems and mottoes appear on practically all the coins of the later world, either permanently or for considerable periods during the country's history.

Thus, broadly, were coins evolved. More detail will be given in succeeding chapters. Thus the spread of coins began, and as each country or nation awoke to civilisation, or had it thrust upon it by others, so the need for coins arose and they developed following the same broad outline. Gaps in the outline occur here and there; in some instances coinage development was only reached at second or third hand but, in the main, coins followed the track of civilisation as it spread over the world.

Broadly speaking, the development of a nation's coinage can be said to depend on the following. (*a*) The contact of the nation or group of people concerned with other nations or groups of peoples of a higher standard of civilisation. (*b*) The extent of the territories of the nation concerned. (*c*) The means of transport available to that nation. As we progress from foot to horse, from carriage to mechanical vehicles, from galley to deep-sea ship, so territories expand and the force of items (*a*) and (*b*) come into play over a wider circle. (*d*) The internal wealth of the nation. On this the actual evolution of a nation's coins depends.

Very often coinages progress from base metals to precious metals, as base metals become more easily obtained and more common while each civilisation proceeds and values change. Then, in almost all cases, a period of decline sets in, during which coins pass from the precious metal stage back to base metals. By then a nation can be said to be facing economic bankruptcy so long as its neighbours are still in a position to continue to use precious metals for coinage purposes. This takes no account of banknotes and paper money, which are outside the scope of this book and which, unless backed by a store of precious metals, are of even less value than a base metal coin.

This cycle of events is worthy of more comment, since those who study coins will find that it constantly recurs. There have been numerous examples within our own times.

Since the time when countries and nations came to depend for survival on trade rather than on conquest, and to be ruled by Parliaments and Democracies rather than by Emperors and Kings, no nation has wholly passed away. The system of democracy based on international commerce has not been in use long enough for this to happen. When it does, not one nation but many will be dragged down together into oblivion. In a world ruled by commerce, it is more in a nation's interest to sustain its neighbours as an outlet for its own trade than to see them perish.

This does not stop nations and countries passing through periods of financial depression or bankruptcy. Such a state may continue for many years till such time as some new invention or some urgently required natural resource is discovered. With this to stimulate trade, the financial fortunes of a nation and its position in world power commence to rise.

These economic cycles are at once reflected in the coinage. From a high level of prosperity, first the standard of the coinage is debased by increasing the amount of alloy in the metal from which the coins are produced. The metallic value of the coin is no longer its exchange value. Then the use of precious metal for coins begins to disappear till its use ceases altogether. More paper money, unbacked by bullion, goes into circulation; cheaper metals are used for the coins. Finally, the country exists on a purely token coinage, the intrinsic value of each coin being negligible. To what depths a country may sink at this point in the cycle can be studied in the history of the German coinage after the First World War.

In Britain's case, having sustained the brunt of two world wars the coinage has now reached the token stage. As though to disprove the above statements, the country is prosperous and the standard of living high. The reason for the token coinage at present in use is, basically, that the Government, having borrowed money and incurred great financial obligations during the Second World War, repaid borrowed silver and gold in kind. The source of much of the silver was in the coinage itself, which was melted down and exported. When the final debt is paid one hopes it may be possible to return to a precious metal coinage. This may be possible if inflation and falling trade balances do not occur, thus completing the cycle of events.

Though no silver coins have been minted since 1946, some millions of sovereigns have been struck in recent years. These, however, are not for circulation but are in the main intended to familiarise certain Eastern countries, which still circulate British sovereigns, with the new Queen's coinage. Also large numbers of forged sovereigns, made in Italy and elsewhere, began to make their appearance in countries where the sovereign was still in use, and the new strikings are to counteract such activities.

The sovereigns so struck were not available in Great Britain save to collectors, from coin dealers who had to obtain them from Switzerland, where there is a free gold market, and where they were sold at a high premium above their face value.

Apart from these recent strikings, the unit of our coinage had not been struck for circulation since 1917. A few sovereigns were struck in 1925, but not put into circulation, and a trial minting took place in 1951. This was intended as an 'exercise' to keep the mint workers in touch with the technical processes of gold coin production.

With the repayment of British silver debts in kind and the introduction of cupro-nickel token coins in place of the silver range, only Maundy money, of which more later, continued to be struck in precious metal.

As forecast in the previous edition of this work, the farthing has now been demonetised. It cost more than face value to produce. No pennies were struck between 1953 and 1961, the demand for them not being as great as it was, since they will purchase so little. The Report published by the Royal Mint in 1960, covering mint activities for the year 1959, forecast smaller pennies and halfpennies when the farthing had finally gone.

This forecast will probably come to fruition when the various sizes of the decimal coinage pieces are seen. Smaller coins of these denominations are already in circulation in some parts of the Commonwealth. There are also hints of the possibility of coins from man-made plastics. It has been pointed out that these could be made radio-active, to assist in their being counted by mechanical means. On balance then, it will be seen that we are at present well down the road to a valueless coinage. It is to be hoped that the almost inevitable economic collapse will not follow.

England's fortunes, once based on wool, came, in an increasingly mechanised world, to be based on coal. This could be exported, either in natural form or as manufactured products. Modern industry now obtains the majority of its power from electricity; each factory no longer has to have its own furnace and steam plant. Electricity will soon be increasingly produced by atomic power, and much of our mechanical civilisation turns upon oil, of which Great Britain contains no commercial quantities. It will therefore take the discovery of some entirely new natural product, some exportable supply needed by the world at large, to repair the fortunes of British coinage. Such developments take time. With modern scientific progress they may never occur in this form. Meantime the gap must be bridged by trade in manufactured articles against increasing competition. It may well take a century of progress to put British coinage again on the upward road.

This is but elementary economics, but some understanding of the main points is essential if the full benefit is to be obtained from the study of the science of numismatics. With these basic facts in mind we can now turn to the study of the production of coins themselves.

CHAPTER TWO

How Coins are Made

BEING purely functional objects, coins have adopted the most natural shape suitable for their purpose. In the main they have always been circular, but there are other shapes with which the numismatist comes into contact. In practically every case, if a coin is not circular its deviation from the normal is for a functional reason.

The earliest coins which are known to us do not subscribe to this rule, though the intention, more by accident than design, is there. They are irregular in shape, being little more than small metallic lumps, roughly impressed with a form of counter-stamp. The true circle, being the most difficult form to obtain, eluded the early coiners, but the impressing of the counter-stamp on the heated lumps of metal tended to give them, if not a circular, at least an oval form, and as Greek coinage developed these lumps soon began to take a more circular shape. From that time forward this has been maintained as the main shape to which coins conform. From ancient times coinage reflects a constant struggle on the part of the mints to obtain this circular shape, an even thickness and a constant denominational weight. It took some three hundred years of machine-made coins before these conditions could all be satisfied for 100 per cent production from any mint.

The manufacture of coins is basically a twofold operation; the preparation of the flan or blank, and the striking of the device on the flan so prepared. The two principal ways of making coins are by striking and casting. Of these the first is the more usual method. The latter is mainly in evidence during the primitive stage of coin development in a civilised community, and for the production of forgeries of true coins. At times the methods overlap, both being in use at once.

The Romans passed through the casting stage of coin production, as did the Ancient British. Certain Early British issues of 'tin', *circa* 100–75 B.C., appear to have been cast in lengths in wooden moulds, the coins being separated by breaking after cooling. Casting in bulk for later separation was used in China for small denomination coins till comparatively recent times.

The production of coins by casting has certain obvious drawbacks which proved great obstacles in primitive times. Flaws and air bubbles form in the metal, causing the coins to break; the device on the coin may not turn out fully completed; coins of varying thickness and weight may result. As coinage develops this method is soon discarded in favour of a two-stage production.

Before the machine age these stages were of simple form. A sheet of metal was prepared and hammered as far as possible to a uniform thickness. From these sheets circles of metal were either punched or cut with shears, trimmed to a correct size and weight and then passed to be struck with the device.

Alternatively, a quantity of metal might be made into bars, roughly the same diameter as the coins. The blanks were then cut from the bars and trimmed for size and weight. Within the limits of the accuracy of the weighing methods of any particular age, very little difference was allowed between the weight of any coin and its counterpart, since the value of true coins is fixed by the weight and fineness of the metal used.

The blanks prepared, they were passed to the striker. He was provided with two previously cut metal dies, representing each side of the coin. That for the obverse was usually placed firmly in a block of wood, and from earliest times it became an almost fixed custom that the obverse die should always be the lower at the moment of striking, a custom which still holds. It developed from observing the fact that the die which was struck by the hammer lasted for a shorter time than the lower die.

The blank having been placed on the lower die, the upper die was placed in contact with it and was struck a sharp blow with a hammer. If one blow was not enough, further striking was given. This sometimes resulted in marred coins, referred to as double struck. Anyone who has tried to print twice on exactly the same spot with a rubber stamp will know that it is next to impossible without fixed guides in which the stamp can run. The result obtained is exactly that of a double-struck coin. Some dies had side walls into which the upper die fitted, thus being held in place. Others were held in place by pegs, and yet a third type were hinged together to ensure accurate centring.

From this it will be seen that the method of producing coins made it almost impossible for the true circle to be obtained, since there was little to stop the flan from spreading under the blow. The use of a type of collar for the flan, an idea which developed in due course, often caused the metal to thicken at the edges or to turn up in a rim.

Here again it took many years of the mechanical age before the size of the blank, the force of the blow and the compression of the collar could all be related in such a way as to produce a perfectly circular coin every time.

The production of dies is an intricate process. It is customary to speak of dies as being engraved, but such is not always the case. Early English dies were usually made by building up the design by punching it into the face of the metal with a series of punches. Some of the earliest examples of this type of die-making can be seen in the English silver pennies of the period *circa* A.D. 800–1300. A study of the lettering will show that each letter is built up by the use of two or more punches. A punch-shaped () did duty for an upright stroke or a horizontal bar. Another, shaped ⌓, was used to produce a rough letter S, and so on. Similarly, the effigy of the ruler was built up from a series of suitable punches, which produced a very creditable human face even if it bore little likeness to the king himself.

The process of growth from this stage was gradual and obvious. Punches with complete letters or complete words were developed, and by the time of Henry VII (1485–1509) a complete portrait of the king was contained on a single punch.

As soon as machinery began to be developed for minting coins, progress was more rapid. For a long time dies were still cut by hand, but the invention of the reducing machine, originally a German idea, altered the process of die-making. To produce a modern die a large plaster cast, about 18 inches in diameter, is made of the whole of the design for one side of the coin. A plated copy of this is made in metal and placed in the reducing machine. This machine, working on the pantograph principle, then produces a smaller replica. This is then replaced in the machine, which is altered to suit the new smaller model. A cutting edge on the other end of the pantograph arm than cuts out a master punch of the design to the correct size of the coin, being guided in its action by the tracing finger at the opposite end of the arm, which follows faithfully the design and contour of the model. When this punch, known as the reduction punch, is complete, it is used to produce an incuse matrix, from which in turn the coin dies are prepared. This process enables large numbers of exactly similar dies to be produced to meet the modern demand for several millions of the same coin. Since dies can now be made to last some 100,000 strikings before needing to be replaced, and since many of the more common coins are struck several millions to the year, the advantages of this method of die production are patent. With the beginning of a new year, the last figure of the date is removed from one of the working punches and a new matrix is made into which the new figure or figures are cut. From this the process then follows, new working punches and dies being prepared. On occasions it is possible to see that the final figure of a date has been altered, but though this was not uncommon in the earlier years of mechanical coin production it is now a very rare occurrence.

The hammered coin and its method of minting gave rise to many slight variations, which are definitely of academic interest. Considerable attention has been paid to them by many numismatists and they continue to be a constant study.

It will have been gleaned from what has been said so far that the various mints through the mediæval world were faced with the constant menace of clipped coins, forged coins and coins illegally struck. Since in any one country hammered coins were rarely perfectly true in shape; since their weight varied slightly and since various mints, both regal and operating under royal licence or patent, increased the number and type of coin in circulation, the way was wide open to the clipper and forger. In spite of the drastic penalties imposed, such people were not slow to take every advantage offered. Methods were therefore constantly sought to eliminate such evils, which in some cases became so prevalent as to threaten the economic stability of the country concerned. Some of the best brains of the Middle Ages were concerned with the problem, and over the whole of Europe it was being tackled in various ways.

Another great evil which faced most countries was the export of home coinage to other countries where it had an enhanced value, and the imitation of home coinage by other countries, who put such imitations into circulation, causing considerable confusion among illiterate populations. These two evils, particularly the former, have lasted till our own times. Many will know of the enhanced value of the few remaining English sovereigns in foreign countries during the Second World War. The appearance of large numbers of forged sovereigns in Europe in the 1950's has just been referred to in the last chapter. Only the partial answer to some of the problems created by forgery came with machine-made coins.

As far as can be ascertained, the process of striking coins and medals by machinery had its origin in Italy. The earliest examples of the art and experiments with the process seem to have been associated mainly with the production of medals commemorating some person or historical event. Experiments were carried on in various places. One of the first names on record as being associated with the use of the screw-coining press is that of Bramante (1444–1514). He was an eminent architect and painter and a relative of Raphael. It will come as no surprise that the genius of Leonardo da Vinci (1452–1519) was bent to the problem. Towards the end of his life he devised a mechanical means of producing and striking coin blanks, probably during the period when he is said to have been associated with the mint at Rome, in about the year 1514.

Another historic name linked with the mint at Rome is that of Benvenuto Cellini, who was appointed engraver in 1529. He was closely associated with the mill and screw method of coining, and produced a treatise on the whole subject of milled and hammered coins in 1558.

In 1537 Cellini visited France, and the matter was discussed between the artist and Francis I, though no material result appears to have emanated therefrom at that time. Henry II, Francis's son, appears to have recalled these discussions at a later date. He and his administration were faced with the problem of coinage reform, as forgery and clipping had assumed alarming proportions and were gradually undermining the economic stability of the State. Henry therefore obtained from Augsburg various machines for striking coins and they were set up in the grounds of the palace in 1552, when proof coins were struck with success. It is probably from this installation that the milled series of coins originally takes its name.

Some years after, Henry of Navarre, later the famous Henry IV of France, caused similar machinery to be installed at Pau, his birthplace.

Two developments had proceeded side by side. They were the production of machines to roll out the metal into an even thickness, and the manufacture of a machine to stamp out blanks from the flat strips of metal, with another to strike the design on the blanks so produced.

It will be realised that some source of power to drive the rolling mills was needed, and for this purpose wind, water and horse-mills were employed. From this comes the term 'milled coinage', since at a certain stage in its production the coin passed 'through the mill'. It has come to be popularly supposed that a coin with a number of teeth on its edge is by reason of such markings a milled coin, but this is not so. The toothed edge is more properly termed a grained edge. Any coin, whether it has a grained, lettered, grooved or plain edge, is a milled coin if it is produced by means of the mechanical mill.

The stage was now set for the introduction of the mill method of coin production to be introduced into England. Not only was the necessary machinery available, but the English administration, faced with vast quantities of clipped and base coins, had, like the administration of France, to take drastic steps towards coinage reform. In 1561 Mestrell, who as far as can be ascertained was an employee of the French mint, arrived in London and was employed at the Tower Mint. There is little doubt that he was instrumental in introducing something of the new methods of coining, but these found little favour with the Tower Mint authorities. Though many milled Elizabethan coins are still in existence the process was discontinued after 1572, and Mestrell appears to have been hanged at Tyburn about 1578 for counterfeiting.

Little now seems to have been done in the matter till 1633. In that year Nicholas Briot (1579–1646) was appointed Chief Engraver at the Royal Mint, and he set about improving the mechanical method of coin production. Many examples of his work are still in existence. Unfortunately, he was in office during a time of national unrest, which retarded peaceful improvements as wars always will. During the latter part of the Civil War Briot retired to Oxford, where he died.

Coinage reform was not lost sight of, and during the period of the Commonwealth the Government again took the matter in hand. At the Royal Mint Ramage was experimenting, no doubt with the machinery left by Briot and his predecessors, and in 1649 the Government invited Peter Blondeau over from France. Though before the days of the Trade Union movement, those employed at the Royal Mint made every effort to freeze Blondeau out, with the result that Warrants were issued to both Ramage and Blondeau, under the terms of which they had to prepare patterns of milled coins for the consideration of the Council.

Though the main improvements which Blondeau carried out in connection with milled coins were mainly concerned with the markings of the edges, a sure safeguard against clipping, comparison of the coins produced under the Warrants will show that his patterns were superior to those of Ramage. However, the opposition proved too strong for him, and he resigned from the Royal Mint in 1656 and returned to France with a pension of £100.

The few milled coins which were struck during the Protectorate of Cromwell were probably struck on the machines which Blondeau left. Through inexperience on the part of the operatives damage was caused to the dies, particularly of the crown.

The matter was finally settled by Charles II and his administration. After the Restoration (1660) Blondeau was invited back to this country, and appointed Provost of the moneyers and engravers at the Royal Mint at the Tower. This post he held for fourteen years, his agreement stating that he was to 'furnish all mills, rollers, presses, and other instruments, to cut, flatten, make round and size the pieces: the engines to mark the edges of the money with letters and grainings, the great presses for the coinage of monies, and all other tools and engines for the new way of coining'. He also engaged 'to discover his secrets in rounding pieces before they are seized, and in marking the edges of the monies'.

Though during the first two years of his reign, while the above events were in train, Charles issued hammered coins, a clear-cut decision was arrived at, and in 1662 it was ordained that in future only milled coins should be struck. This sounded the knell of the hammered coin in England, and although pieces of this type continued to circulate along with the new money, they were finally demonetised in 1696. All remaining hammered coins were then withdrawn from circulation, and by this time most of the surviving pieces were in a very poor condition. The cost of financing this withdrawal of poor coin and its replacement by new was partly defrayed by a Window Tax. This was in the reign of William III (1694–1702), though the decision might well have been arrived at earlier but for the unrest during the reign of James II (1685–88).

With the signing of Blondeau's agreement a competition was entered into between the chief engraver of the Mint, Thomas Simon, and John Roettier, of Antwerp, to decide who should make the dies for the new coinage. Roettier's patterns were preferred and he was entrusted with the work. During his exile in the Low Countries Charles II had met Roettier's family, and promised certain of them employment in England when he should be restored to the throne.

We have now arrived at the stage where all English money was produced by mechanical means, from bars of metal rolled to a uniform thickness, struck in manually operated coin presses. These presses consisted of a device not unlike a letter-copying press on a large scale. The obverse die was placed in the bedplate, two or four men with lines attached to the capstan above the screw gave a sharp turn, bringing down the reverse die into contact with the preplaced coin blank, thus producing the coin.

The edges of all the new coins were marked, since they were now of sufficient thickness to allow this. Usually a legend appeared, such as DECUS ET TUTAMEN (an ornament and a safeguard [against clippers]), and the regnal year of the monarch. Other coins were marked with various styles of graining. Though not all the coins were absolutely circular, since dies cracked or broke, flans and edge collars sprang out of position, or the flan cracked slightly at the edge under the blow of striking, a tremendous step forward had been made. Clipping was now almost impossible and forgery showed a decline.

Coinage proceeded along these lines during the reigns of James II (1685–88), William and Mary (1688–94), William III (1694–1702), Anne (1702–14), George I (1714–27), George II (1727–60), and part of the reign of George III (1760–1820). The stage was by then set for the next major improvement in the art of coining, the introduction of mass production, of the steam-engine as a source of power and of improved presses and rollers.

Contrary to what is generally supposed, even today, James Watt did not invent the steam-engine. In its most primitive form it was known to the Ancient Greeks: they not only saw in it a very early form of jet propulsion, but used its powers, in a very elementary way, literally to 'work the oracle'. Steam-power was used by them to cause oracular figures to move in some of the Greek temples, to make doors open on command, and in general to impress the members of the public who came to consult the oracle.

In the intervening centuries the knowledge seems to have been almost lost, and it is not until 1712 that it made a reappearance. This time it was in a far more practicable form than the Greeks had dreamed of, and its discoverer was Thomas Newcomen. He little suspected that he was to lay the foundation upon which industrial civilisation was soon to be based.

Newcomen's engines were utilised for the purpose of pumping water out of mines, and it was not until 1763 that Watt, asked to repair a model of the Newcomen atmospheric steam-engine belonging to the Natural Philosophy Class in the College of Glasgow, began seriously to experiment with the steam-engine.

Watt continued his experiments and improvements, and in 1768 journeyed to London to secure a patent for a device he had evolved in connection with steam-engines. On his way back to the north he broke his journey at Birmingham to visit Matthew Boulton at Soho House.

Thus an almost chance meeting was to influence the course of history in a way that can probably never be measured.

Boulton, one of the best-known manufacturers in the Midlands, had succeeded to his father's business, that of a silver stamper and piercer. This business he soon extended by adding the manufacture of steel, gilt and fancy buttons, steel watch-chains and sword hilts, plated wares, ornamental works in ormolu, and tortoise-shell and steel buckles.

Boulton may be said to be the father of mass production. He gave birth to the idea later extended by Henry Ford. At this time factories as we know them did not exist. Various forms of hardware were produced in a large number of small workshops, and Boulton's factory, employing some 600 workmen, laid the foundation of modern factory practice.

Obviously such a concern needed a considerable supply of power. The very position of the Soho manufactory was due to the fact that the site on which it grew up was traversed by the Hockley Brook which, suitably dammed, acted as the power supply.

Plate 1 GREEK COINS

1. Tetradrachm of Athens, archaic style.
2. Stater of Corinth.
3. Gold Stater of Philip of Macedon.
4. Gold Stater of Alexander the Great of Macedon.
5. Stater of Metapontum.
6. Stater of Tarentum.

Plate 1

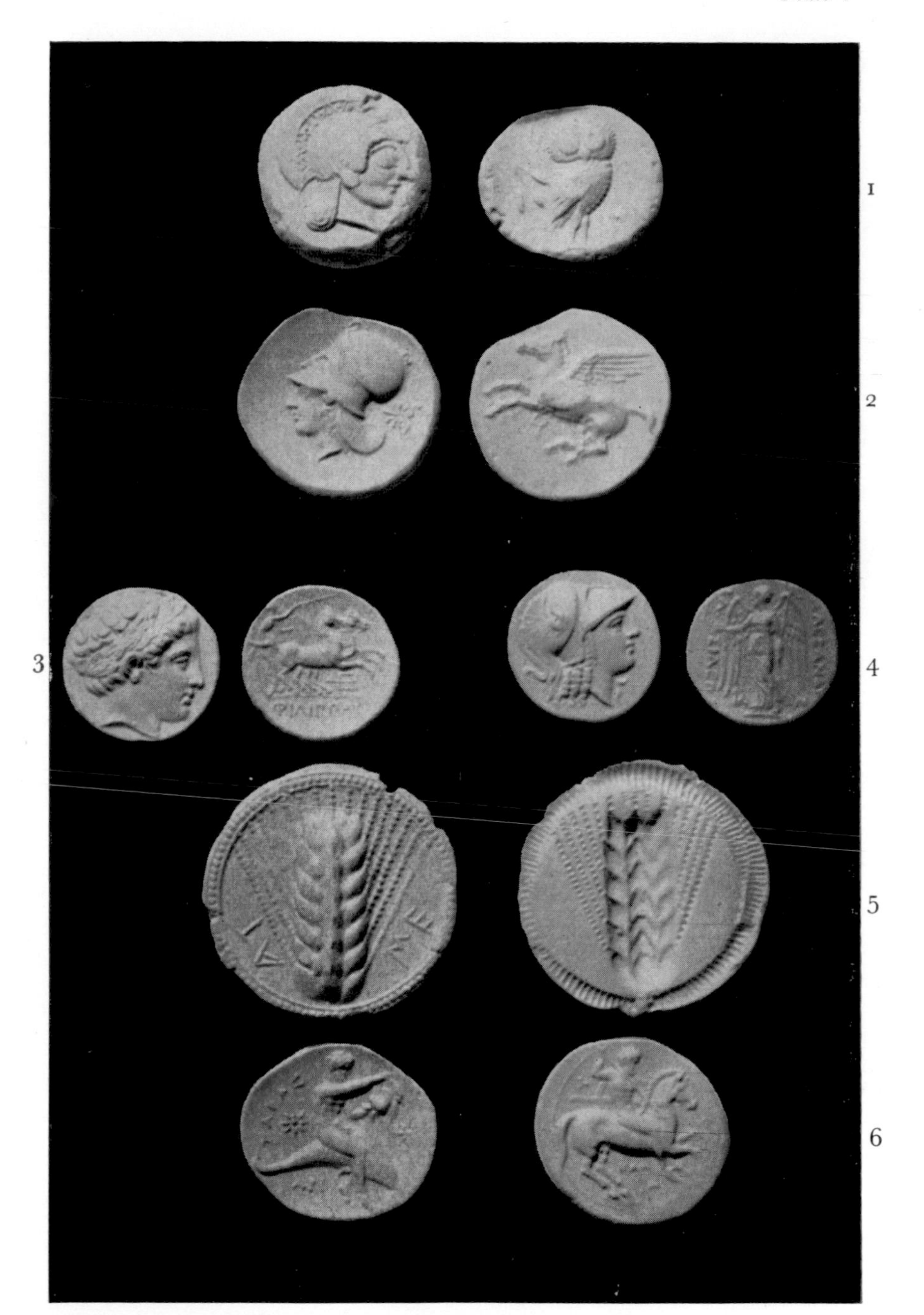

Plate 2

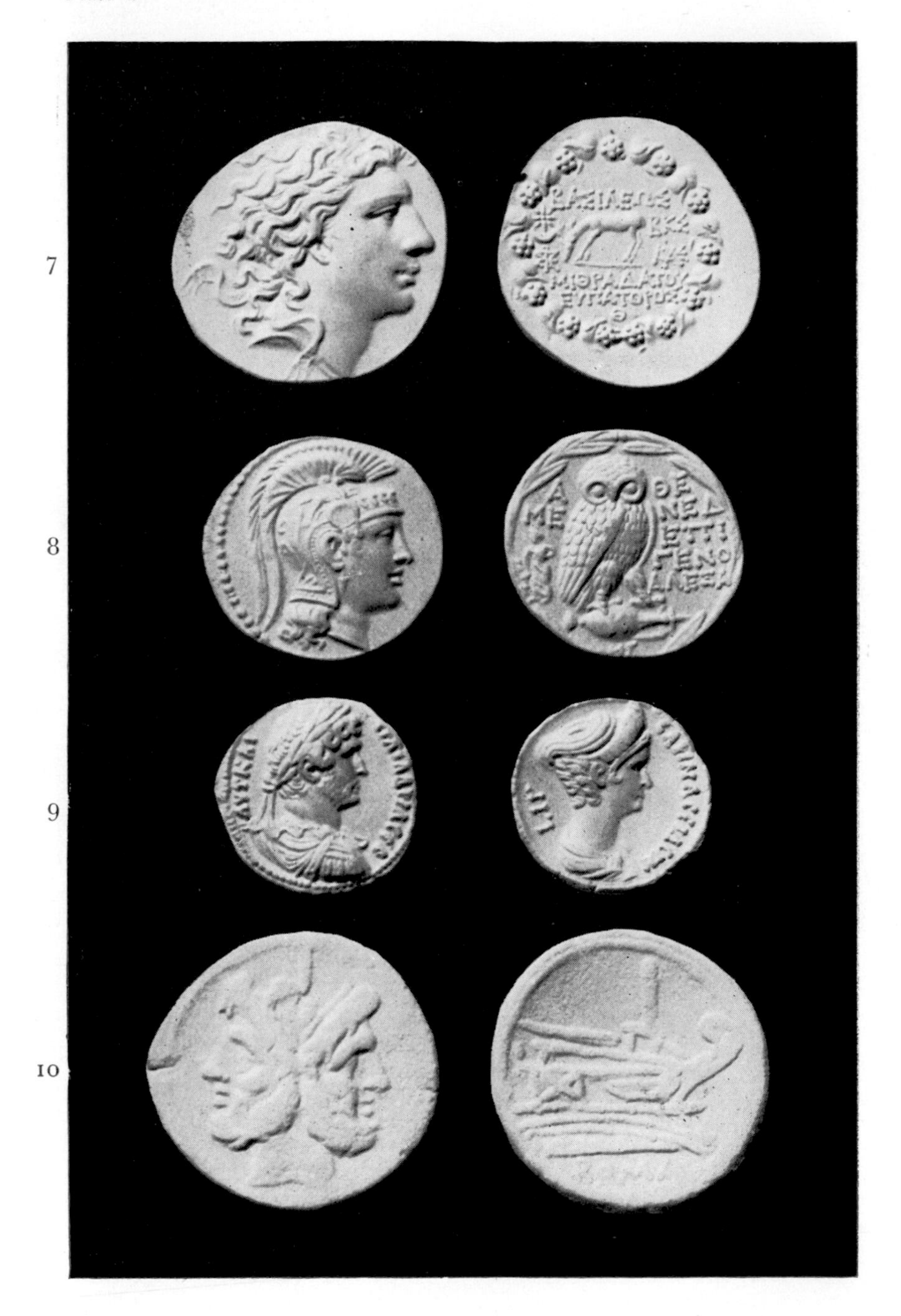

In partnership with Watt, Boulton realised that the steam-engine could be harnessed to drive the machines of his works. Apart from this, business eventuated from the supply of mine-pumping engines, in which the partners built up a very thriving line. It was but a step to the production of a range of steam-engines, suitable for general power supply.

Boulton and Watt began considering the application of steam-power to the art of coining in about 1774. With a steam-powered factory at their command it was a natural development. There had long been a demand in the country for a copper coinage. It found an expression in the seventeenth century, as will be seen, by the issue of copper tokens by all classes of traders. Later, Royal licences were granted for the manufacture of small denominations of copper coins. Gradually, through the reigns of the later Stuarts, the House of Orange and the House of Hanover, a copper coinage began to be an established part of the country's monetary system.

In quantity it was not adequate for the demand. During the Napoleonic wars little coinage was issued save gold. Extraordinary measures had to be taken to provide silver specie.

Plate 2 GREEK AND ROMAN COINS

7. Tetradrachm of Mithridates the Great.
8. Tetradrachm of Athens, 'new' style.
9. Billion Tetradrachm of Alexandria, showing Hadrian and his wife, Sabina.
10. An As.

Copper rose in value by 100 per cent, so that a proper coinage in this metal was again delayed. At this period the Boulton and Watt partnership matured, in a numismatic sense, with startling results.

Boulton knew that the intrinsic value of a coin and the accuracy of its manufacture should be such that counterfeiting would no longer be worth while. By improvements in existing machines, by planned and co-ordinated production and by the application of steam-power, Boulton saw that this object could be achieved.

He took up the question with all his characteristic vigour. He erected at Soho some of the best coining presses then available, and with them struck some 100 tons of copper coinage for the Honourable East India Company. At this period Indian trade was completely in the hands of this Company, who developed what was to become the Indian Empire and who issued their own coinage for the purposes of their trade.

In 1788 Boulton was invited to appear before a Committee of the Privy Council, where he expounded his views to such good effect that he was invited to submit pattern coins, halfpennies, struck on his new industrial plan. He offered to execute the coinage of halfpennies for the Government at a cost of not more than half that incurred by the Royal Mint, and though the offer was not then taken up and the matter rested, Boulton was not idle. He erected further new coining presses in a building which was afterwards known as the Soho Mint. He employed the best artists and die-cutters to produce the necessary dies, and the whole scheme was ready for action by 1788. With the general improvements went the plant for rolling the copper ingots, multiplying the dies, and doing all that was necessary to provide a coinage of absolutely accurate size and weight. Though he applied methods already known in this, his own genius for organisation showed itself in that he not only improved the machines, but arranged them in such a way that the various processes followed in an ordered sequence, one machine feeding the next so that no machine stood idle, waiting on others. Handling was cut to a minimum.

With this equipment he executed a copper coinage for the American Colonies and a silver coinage for the Sierra Leone

Company. He thus founded a type of mint where the minimum number of operations could produce the maximum number of accurate coins.

So far as the Government of the day was concerned, nothing was done to alleviate the hardships imposed upon the country by the lack of small change. Local firms and private individuals were again forced to issue coinages of their own, while Boulton exhorted the Government to remedy the deficiency in the national coinage, and incidentally give his factory work.

Much of the manufacture of private tokens fell upon Boulton. He and the perfection of the coins which he produced combined to good effect. So well did he execute his various colonial and private contracts that the Government, at last forced into action, awarded him the contract for the striking of regal copper coinage.

This was to consist of a coinage of 20 tons of twopenny-pieces and 480 tons of penny-pieces, at a price of £108 a ton. These coins made their appearance in 1797 and large numbers of them are still in existence. When compared with other coins of the period they are a practical testimony to Boulton's genius. In this way Boulton and Watt between them were partly responsible for the accuracy with which coins are struck today.

Further contracts for coinage were awarded to Boulton, till at last the Royal Mint, realising both the antiquity of its equipment and the inadequacy of its situation, was moved from its traditional place in the Tower of London to its present site on Tower Hill. Boulton was employed to help plan the edifice and supply and erect the necessary machinery, including the steam-engines required for motive-power. This triumph for the first great industrialist took place in 1805–10. The result, though primitive to modern eyes, was looked upon as the most complete mint in the world, and the machinery was not superseded till 1881–82. Boulton also influenced the coinage of various foreign countries, by supplying machinery for a number of continental mints. Russia, buying a set of his machinery in 1799, was the first state to own plant for coining by steam.*

Something of Boulton's achievements in the field of coinage are summed up by Darwin, who says of him: 'Mr. Boulton

* Cf. Craig: *The Mint.*

has lately constructed at Soho near Birmingham, a most magnificent apparatus for Coining which has cost him some thousand pounds; the whole machinery is moved by an improved steam-engine, which rolls the copper for halfpence finer than copper has before been rolled for the purpose of making money; it works the coupoirs or screw-presses for cutting out the circular pieces of copper; and coins both faces and edges of the money at the same time, with such superior excellence and cheapness of workmanship, as well as with marks of such powerful machinery as must totally prevent clandestine imitation, and in consequence save many lives from the hand of the executioner; a circumstance worthy the attention of a great minister. If a civic crown was given in Rome for preserving the life of one citizen, Mr. Boulton should be covered with garlands of oak. By this machinery four boys of ten or twelve years old are capable of striking thirty thousand guineas in an hour, and the machine itself keeps an unerring account of the pieces struck.'

But by 1881 the equipment and the methods of Boulton had gone out of date. At this period of the Industrial Revolution power was conveyed from its source to some other point by gears and levers. Belt-driven machinery and the transmission of power by belt drive had not yet progressed far enough to be of use for heavy work. One must imagine the coining presses and rolling mills of the Royal Mint being driven through great gears, and levers which nodded slowly up and down against the ceiling, through gaps in walls and over corridors and passages.

Further, one of the main features of the Boulton coin press was that the coin was struck a heavy blow, so that the whole building shook under the impact. In the intervening years a coining press working on a different principle had been evolved. Invented in 1839, installed in the French mints in 1845 and in the branch Royal Mints at Sydney and Melbourne in 1853 and 1869, the new press exerted heavy and steady pressure, obtaining the same result without the heavy blow of the Boulton press.

These Uhlhorn presses made slow but steady entry into use at the Royal Mint between 1872 and 1878. More of these and other improvements might have been carried out had the subject of the removal of the Mint to a new site not been under consideration. Finally, a decision against removal was given, and the mint, after striking £500,000 of silver coins to cover the period and sub-contracting bronze and colonial coins, closed down in February 1882 for a refit.

New buildings and machinery were erected and installed, and from that time onward fairly steady progress has been maintained in keeping abreast of modern inventions and improvements. One of the latest rebuilding schemes was undertaken in 1924, but without a stoppage of work. Quite recently high-frequency electric furnaces of the latest type were installed for dealing with the alloy, cupro-nickel, from which British 'silver' coins are now made.

With the machinery, technicians and modern developments at its command, the annual output of coins by the Royal Mint for Great Britain, for the Commonwealth and for foreign governments reaches thousands of millions of pieces each year.

After this brief survey of the making of coins, we can now turn our attention to some aspects of a subject of further interest to the numismatist, that of coin collecting.

CHAPTER THREE

On Collecting Coins

Most people at some time or other feel the urge to collect. Why this is so is not easy to discover. In many cases it would appear to be an outlet for a form of affection, coupled with a sense of pride of possession. Thus we get people collecting anything from empty tins to old motor-cars; from picture postcards to rare books and manuscripts.

Whatever the form of the collection, it is not long before the art of appreciation becomes apparent, and with it comes the full value of the collection to the collector.

So with many who collect coins. Before long the collection, often begun with some apparently worthless specimens, begins to take a definite shape, based upon whatever aspect of appreciation may appeal to the collector. Probably the most common is that of an appreciation of some part of history, the artistic merit of certain types of coins; of the ruler or government which issued them; of the country from which they came, or of the very metal from which they are made. Not to be over-looked is the appreciation in value of the collection from an investment point of view. This may well become considerable if a collection is formed with care and judgement.

With most numismatists an interest in history or archaeology is a natural incentive to, or result from, the formation of their collections. The importance of numismatics in the study of history is only of recent years being fully realised, though there is, as yet, no Chair of Numismatics in an English University.

The reasons why any individual starts to collect coins are as diverse as they are numerous. With some it will begin with an odd, perhaps quite valueless coin, passed on by a friend or found in some forgotten corner. With another it may start with the purchase of an already considerable collection, to which the collector will go on adding coin after coin throughout his collecting life. From a review of the great collectors of the past one thing is clear: no great knowledge, no considerable erudition is necessary before the formation of a coin collection is undertaken. The simplest of interests at the beginning will eventually bring with it all the knowledge and erudition which the collector may wish to acquire. All knowledge is an asset, and people in almost every walk of life have, by the pursuit of a hobby, become scholars of considerable distinction and learning as they have built up and studied their collection.

It will at once be appreciated that the whole field of numismatics is vast. Coins have been minted for some thousands of years, so that the field which they cover and the knowledge which has been amassed cannot be compressed within the covers of any one book. There is no handy, quick-reference work which can cover so large a field. It has always been necessary for the collector to break down the subject into a number of very broad sections and, within this framework, to specialise in whatever may take his fancy.

From this standpoint it may be well to illustrate something of the broad sections into which the subject can usefully be divided. There is no definite rule in this matter. The following is simply a series of headings which have evolved naturally with the years as the interests of thousands of collectors have been studied and analysed.

Classical coins, those of Ancient Greece and Rome, form an obvious subdivision. There are many collectors who specialise in only one of these ancient series. Though Greek coins are paramount for those who appreciate artistic merit as well as classical history, the Roman series offers much the wider field, both in variety of specimen and in historical background. Much original research has been and still remains to be done in this section alone.

To whatever country a collector may belong, it is natural that the coins of his country rank high in interest with him, particularly if the series can be traced back some thousand years. British coins, therefore, form a large section, within which many collectors have specialised in one or more aspects.

Great Britain, in common with most of the countries of Europe, possesses a fine range of silver crown pieces,* dating

* See the author's *Crown Pieces of Great Britain and the British Commonwealth*, London, 1962.

back to 1551. In Germany and Austria large ranges of such pieces were coined over the centuries. Many of them have most interesting pictorial reverse designs, showing cities, early mines and machinery, battles, and so forth. Switzerland is famous for a long series of Talers commemorating shooting events, a series still being struck, while the Spanish Eight Reales piece (the 'Pieces of Eight' of pirate stories) has a history long enough to fill several volumes. Many collectors specialise in coins of this size and type alone, and they are indeed a most satisfactory series on which to concentrate.*

Though not yet old in numismatic time, the coins of the Commonwealth of Nations, the British Dominions, Colonies and Protectorates, are a series in which the collector of more modern coins will find an interest. Particularly so if he has had the good fortune to visit or become familiar with some of the countries of which the Commonwealth is comprised.*

From the standpoint of the British collector, all coins outside the Commonwealth can, with typical insularity, be classified as foreign. Here again there is obviously a vast series, which must at once be broken down into constituents in which to specialise. Every country has its own long series of coins, and an appreciation of some historical aspect of any one of the countries concerned under this heading is necessary if the British collector is to specialise in the coins of some country overseas.

A subdivision of the numismatic history of most of the older countries is that of the issues of tokens. These have appeared with fairly constant repetition, often under something like the economic conditions outlined at the end of Chapter One. In this country in particular there is a very considerable series, issued during the seventeenth, eighteenth and nineteenth centuries. They appeal to the collector with a strong taste for local history and an interest in local trades, and they are one of the least expensive types of piece to collect.

Two other forms of money collections exist, that of bank-notes and curious currencies. Of the former there are a growing number of collectors in Britain, but this form of collection does not come within the scope of our work.

Curious currencies are a study in themselves. They consist

* See the author's *British Commonwealth Coinage*, London, 1959.

of almost anything which has served as money without actually being coin in the recognised form. Such things as shells, coal, leather, teeth, stones and beads, to mention only a few, serve or have served the purpose of money.

Finally, there is the series of Commemorative Medals in which collectors are showing a welcome increase of interest. Again these appear in large numbers in most of the older countries. They record in metallic form outstanding events in a country's history. Generally they are highly allegorical in their representations, and an interest in this form of historical presentation, together with that of artistic merit, goes with their collecting. Their greater size offers more scope for portraiture than is possible with the smaller coins.

The problem of how to house a collection arises as soon as a number of specimens is obtained. Its solution must, to some extent, rest with the requirements of the collector. The least expensive method is that of keeping each coin in a small envelope, about two inches square, and then ranking the envelopes in order in a box.

This method is ideal for any collector who may have to spend much of his time travelling about the world and who wishes to carry his collection with him. Apart from this it has few advantages.

A well-tried method is that of keeping the coins in a specially constructed coin cabinet. These vary in size from a cube of about 9-inch sides to a structure as large as a cupboard. In essence they are all fitted in the same way. Within the cabinet are a number of shallow trays, resting on runners. Each tray is pierced with a number of circular holes in each of which a coin is placed. The hole is lined with green baize, and has a smaller hole cut through the base through which the coin can be pushed up from the underside of the tray.

This is probably the ideal method of keeping coins. The cabinet in itself forms an attractive piece of furniture; it can be locked, and the smaller types can be easily stored in a safe or bank when extra security is necessary. Under each coin it is usual to place a circular disc of thin white card, on which any details concerning it can be recorded.

Cabinets of this type are usually made of mahogany, as this

wood contains little natural moisture which would harm the coins. On no account should cedar-wood be used, since it contains a high proportion of natural oil which will spread itself over the coins, to their considerable detriment.

One or two cabinets constructed of man-made plastics have been seen, but so far none have proved satisfactory. The demand for coin cabinets is too small to interest the plastics manufacturers, who thrive on repetition work.

A method of keeping coins which has become popular in recent years, especially in America, is to keep them in a book-form case. This has much to commend it, since the collection can be stored along with ordinary books. The pages of such cases consist of strong, transparent, plastic pages with pockets to hold the coins, and thin card interleaves on which details can be written. The pages are held in a ring-binder. Thus the coins are easily visible and protected from careless handling.

Essentially collectors like to be able to handle their coins readily, and this is only possible with the type of cabinet already described. It will have become obvious from the descriptions given of methods of keeping coins that considerable care is necessary to prevent damage to coins by their contact with each other. Such contact should never be allowed.

Arising out of this is a guiding rule for all collectors. If a coin collection is to keep or appreciate in value, it must consist of specimens in the best possible condition available in the series to which they belong. Care and consideration of this point will give the numismatist a collection of which he can justly be proud, and one which will keep its value.

From this again arises the point of keeping coins clean. As a general rule, a coin which is in good enough condition to be worthy of inclusion in a collection will not need cleaning. Again as a general rule, collector's specimens should not be cleaned, since such action tends to increase wear. On the other hand, coins may have been buried and be very dirty as a result, and silver coins tarnish. If coins must be cleaned, methods should be adopted which necessitate no rubbing of the surface with anything harder than cotton-wool or a soft silver-brush. Such resolvents as lemon juice for gold coins, methylated spirits, ammonia or soapy water for silver, will generally be found to do all that is necessary.

As far as copper coins are concerned, methods of cleaning are much more complicated if the results are to be successful, lasting and non-detrimental to the patina, which most coins of this metal acquire with time. It should not be undertaken without expert advice.

In a general way it will be found that collector's specimens, passing from one collection to another, are well cared for and do not need cleaning. Only in exceptional circumstances should cleaning be undertaken.

In Great Britain there are two old-established Societies, founded to cater for the interests of coin collectors. The senior of these, the Royal Numismatic Society, devotes its attention mainly to the classical series of coins, while the British Numismatic Society, as its name implies, deals more with English and British Commonwealth numismatics, and occasionally with war medals and civil decorations. As well as these two Societies there are an increasing number of local societies and clubs which deal in a less technical manner with the subject. Papers, discussions, exhibitions and debates are a feature of all.

The two learned Societies issue the *Numismatic Chronicle* and the *British Numismatic Journal* respectively, which contain a wealth of information. Some of the other societies and clubs issue their own bulletins and their activities are reported in various numismatic magazines, such as the *Numismatic Circular*. They also hold occasional auctions of Members' coins, and the well-known London auctioneers and a firm of auctioneers in Lewes hold frequent sales of coins throughout the season. Through the established dealers, the auction sales and the clubs, the wealth of numismatic material which the world contains is kept in constant circulation among collectors.

Finally, books of reference on the subject are legion. They deal with every aspect of coin collecting and with every known series. Their field ranges from simple guides for the beginner to the most erudite works on every aspect of all series. Fresh titles appear every month, and to this great library the present work makes its contribution.

But though so much has already been written on the subject

of numismatics, it is far from exhausted. There still remain vast fields for original research for those who are that way inclined. Almost every 'find' of coins brings to light some point worthy of recording. Almost every collection contains the germ of some line of original research.

The British Museum houses the nation's coin collection, which is probably the finest and most representative in the world. Fine collections exist at the Ashmolean Museum at Oxford, the Fitzwilliam Museum at Cambridge, the University of Glasgow, and in Chester, Leeds, Edinburgh, Salisbury, and many provincial museums. These are open to the public, subject to certain informal security measures, and in the case of the larger collections a staff of experts is maintained to carry out research, to maintain the collections and to help and advise. The various museums throughout the world are in close touch in this particular field of science, and material and reports circulate constantly among them. Most local museums contain a collection of coins, often of mainly local interest. Since coins are so easily portable and are not displayed to their best advantage in showcases, it is often necessary to inquire of the Keeper or Curator for permission to consult the collection. To do so is generally taken as indicating that the inquirer is of serious intent, and such inquiries are invariably welcomed.

Having covered the general aspects of collecting, it is now possible to say something of the broader sections into which the science naturally falls. An obvious starting-point is with the classical series, the coinages of Ancient Greece and Rome.

CHAPTER FOUR

Greek Coins

FEW PEOPLE will deny that the coins of Greek cities minted between 680 B.C. and 100 B.C. have the most to offer the collector from the point of view of artistic merit, displayed in a multitude of beautiful obverse and reverse types. It is generally agreed that Ancient Greek coins reached a standard of beauty which has never been approached in any later period. However, many collectors have been frightened away from this fine series of coins because they think that such coins are expensive, and that they themselves lack the knowledge of the Greek language and Greek history which they consider essential for a full appreciation of the coins.

It is quite true that the finest and rarest of Greek coins do command a price beyond the reach of all except a very rich man. For example, there is the magnificent and very rare silver ten-drachma piece of Acragas. This was a wealthy town in Sicily, and the coin was minted at the close of the fifth century B.C., showing on the obverse two eagles tearing at a hare and on the reverse the sun-god driving his chariot. It has realised by private sale several thousands of pounds, while many of the masterpieces in silver of Syracuse, the most famous of Sicilian cities, are constantly being sold for several hundred pounds each. Yet it is quite fair to say that these examples represent only a very small proportion of Greek coins, and specimens of the commoner varieties can be purchased for a pound or so, and occasionally less, and bronze coins of the fourth century B.C. and later for a few shillings only. On the whole, though, there is no denying that Greek coins are generally more expensive than any other series. For his money the collector will be obtaining something which no other series can offer: the pleasure of possessing a coin struck more than two thousand years ago whose beauty can be appreciated even by those of his friends who do not collect coins. Greek coins have an irresistible charm for everyone, while coins of other series tend to remain in the realm of the specialist.

It is entirely owing to the beauty of the coins that the Greek series has become so popular, and so the collector need only know sufficient of the Greek alphabet to be able to read the name of the issuing authority, whether city or king, which on the majority of coins is the only legend which appears. Admittedly, collecting becomes more interesting if one has a knowledge of the history of the particular period, but this knowledge can easily be gained from reading one of the Greek histories designed for use in schools, which can be obtained quite cheaply new or second-hand at most booksellers.

The first step a new collector should take is in the direction of a reputable coin dealer who will be only too willing to guide and advise him. He will find that the coins are sold fully described on a small ticket, and that any additional information, including translation of the legend, will be freely furnished. By subscribing to such a dealer's lists, published periodically, he will form an idea of market prices and so become able to decide what sort of coins will suit his purpose and his pocket.

It is quite impossible in one chapter to trace with any degree of thoroughness the development of Greek coins, and for more scholarly and detailed accounts the reader is referred to the bibliography. A basic outline can, however, be drawn quite simply, with especial reference to the commoner and cheaper coins, specimens of which, with some exceptions, will be found illustrated in Plates 1 and 2.

Greek coins were struck in gold, electrum (a mixture of gold and silver, found naturally alloyed in the rivers and mines of Asia Minor), silver and copper. The question of denominations is complicated by the fact that the commercial value of the coins depended on their weight and basic melting value, and as weight standards differed widely from one group of cities to another, one denomination used in one part of the Greek world is frequently larger and heavier than one current in another. Generally speaking, the unit of currency (*e.g.* in Britain, the pound sterling; in America, the dollar; in France, the franc, etc.) was called the stater. In regions and epochs where the main coinage was of gold, the stater was of gold, but where silver was the main currency the stater was of silver. A further complication is introduced by the fact that the main silver coin of Athens in the fifth century B.C., and hence called the stater, was the piece of four drachms, or tetradrachm, while in Corinth at the same time the main silver coin was a piece of three drachms, technically a tridrachm, but always referred to as a stater. The following table gives some idea of the more common denominations:

Gold. Stater, varying weight, subdivided into denominations of 1/6, 1/12 and 1/24.

Silver. Athens – Tetradrachm (or stater) 264 grains wt.

= 4 drachms
= 8½ drachms (hemidrachm or triobol)
= 12 diobols (6 obols in a drachm)
= 24 obols

Corinth – Stater (132 grains wt.)
= 3 drachms
= 3 Corinthian, or 2 Athenian drachms

In addition to these denominations, there are the dekadrachms (or pieces of ten drachms), an example of which, of Acragas, has already been mentioned, which weigh two and a half times as much as the tetradrachm. These pieces are very rare, and are usually regarded as being medallions given to commemorate some outstanding event and therefore not intended for circulation, though still being struck with reference to the existing weight standard. There also exist double staters in gold struck by Alexander the Great and triple staters of Carthage.

As early as 1100 B.C. electrum was in circulation in the cities of Asia Minor in the shape of small easily-handled 'blobs' of the metal which, of course, had to be weighed in the course of every transaction. At last, about 680 B.C., some rich Lydian or Ionian banker conceived the idea of marking each blob of metal with his own private seal, first having carefully arranged for it to be of a certain weight standard, so that should these particular pieces be returned to him in the course of trade he should not have the bother of reweighing them. Thus the first coin, or money stamped and guaranteed to be of a certain weight, was minted. From this practice, too, came the tradition that each individual issuing authority, city or king, marked its coins with a readily recognisable badge connected with the city. For example, Athens chose for her coins the obverse design of Athena, goddess of the city, and reverse the owl of Athena; Corinth, Pegasus the winged horse, whom Bellerophon the Corinthian hero tamed; Ægina, the sea-turtle, numerous around the shores of that island. The result was that a merchant knew at a glance how much weight and value was represented by the coins of various cities offered to him in the course of trade.

From Asia Minor the new invention of coinage spread to the mainland of Greece, and here Ægina was the first to adopt a currency of her own. This city began about 665 B.C. to issue the coins which have been spoken of above, showing on the obverse the sea-turtle, with the reverse bearing a 'mill-sail' pattern. This latter pattern, which is so frequent on the coins of the sixth and fifth centuries B.C., can hardly be called a design, and was in fact the result of cutting the striking punch so that it would not slip from the blobs of metal when these were being

Plate 3 ROMAN COINS

The Roman coins referred to with their equivalents on p. 55.

11. Semis.
12. Quincunx.
13. Tremis.
14. Quadrans.
15. Sextans.
16. Uncia.

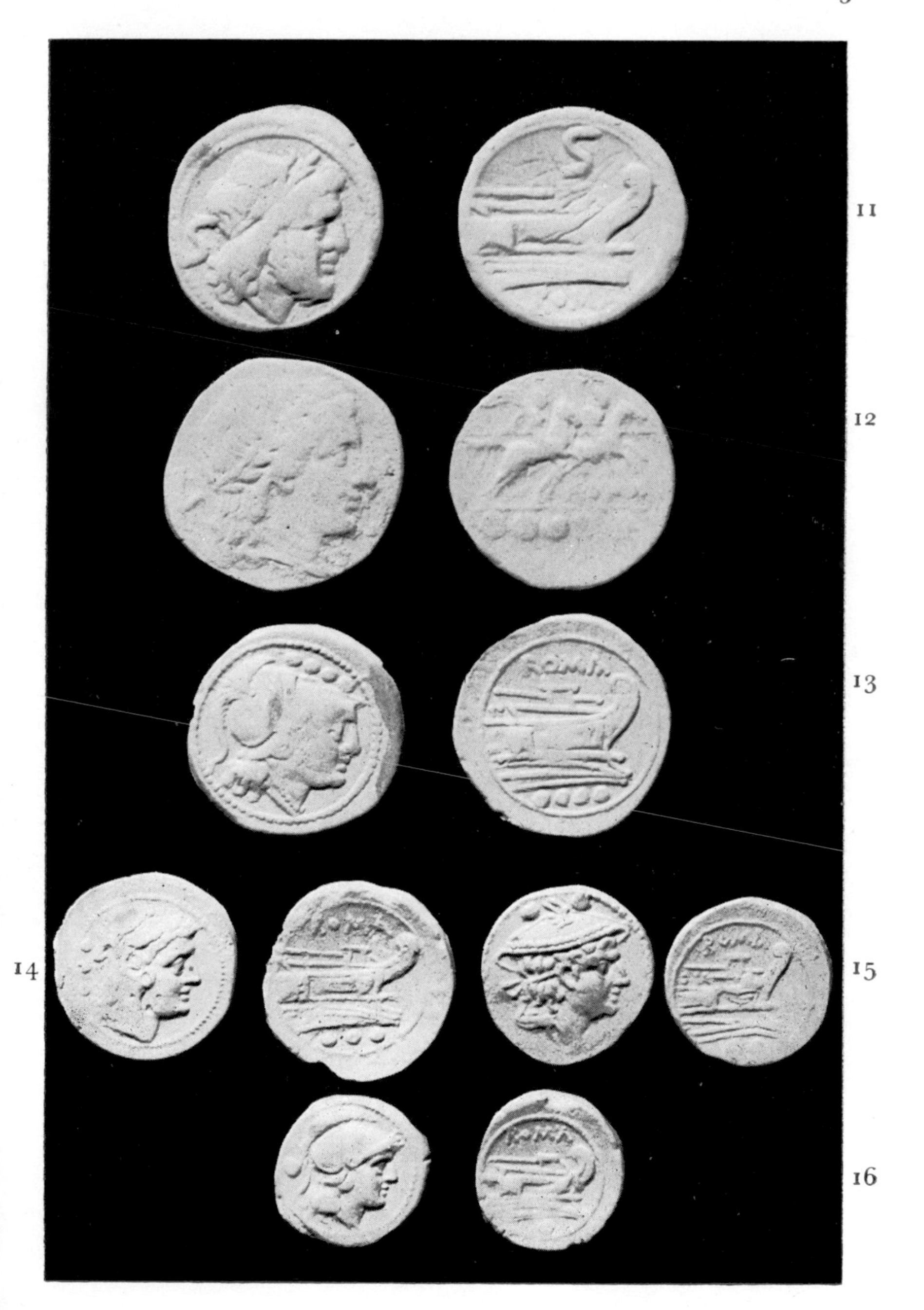
11
12
13
14
15
16

Plate 4

minted. This early period of coinage lasted from about 680 B.C. till about the end of the Persian wars in 480 B.C., and coins struck during this period present a very rough and crude yet fascinating appearance. They are quite naturally scarce and expensive, and not a few collectors, who should know better, mistake their archaic appearance for artistic excellence, forgetting that the art of the engraver and sculptor was then in its infancy.

The fifth and fourth centuries B.C. saw the rapid spread of coinage in Greece, even quite small and unimportant cities issuing their own coins bearing their own device. The coins made rapid advances in beauty and variety of types, and the reverse type soon ceased to represent a mere punch mark and began to embody all the amazing variety of Greek mythology. Athens alone still chose to strike her coins in the old archaic fashion with slight modifications, as if to show the Greek world that Athens was, and would be as powerful and rich as ever.

To this period belongs the remarkable series of silver and gold coins of the rich and powerful cities of Sicily, foremost among which was Syracuse, to whose coins reference has already been

Plate 4 ROMAN COINS

17. A 'Romano-Campanian' Didrachm.
18. Denarius, the reverse showing the two Dioscuri.
19. Denarius, the reverse showing Victory in a biga.
20. Another with reverse showing Jupiter in a quadriga.
21. Another with, on the reverse, the shepherd with the Wolf and Twins.
22. Another, with Juno on the reverse side.
23. A Denarius of Julius Cæsar.
24. A similar coin of Brutus.
25. An Aureus of Hadrian
26. An Aureus quinarius of Commodus.

made. These coins, technically and artistically outstanding in the selection and treatment of their types, are very much sought after by collectors, and it is only those in mediocre condition which can be bought for but a few pounds. However, this period sees the introduction of bronze coinage in many of the cities of the Greek world, and these coins can be purchased quite cheaply. Though not so much care was lavished upon the engraving of their dies, they still reach a high standard of excellence and form an interesting field for collection and study.

When Alexander the Great became King of Macedon in 336 B.C., he introduced silver tetradrachms bearing on the obverse the head of Heracles wearing a lion's skin and on the reverse Zeus, the ruler of the Olympian gods, seated on his throne. The head of Heracles was so unlike the popular idea of this rough and tough hero, and so much like Alexander himself, that Alexander may be considered the first ruler to be portrayed on a coin.

Philip, Alexander's father, had issued enormous quantities of gold staters which circulated far and wide, so much so that the design of the staters of the British tribes in the first century A.D. is believed to have been derived from these coins, which have the head of Apollo for obverse and for reverse a young male figure driving a chariot of two horses. Alexander minted gold staters (obverse type, head of Athena; reverse type, Victory) of the same weight standards as his father, but the silver tetradrachms mentioned above were also related to this standard, so that for the first time gold and silver coins were in circulation with a definite relation to each other, such as, for example, the English sovereign and shilling used to have. Previous to Alexander's time, gold and silver currency were kept quite separate in business transactions, and the gold at least was weighed separately. By the vastness of his empire, Alexander was able to introduce his new coinage over the Greek world and the former Persian Empire and clear the way for a new development of coinage. The tetradrachm of Alexander is one of the commonest of Greek coins, and a good specimen may be bought for a pound or so.

From the sixth century down to the time of the Roman Republic, an important group of cities in Italy, started as Greek colonies, was producing an immense amount of coins. Many of these cities, such as Metapontum, struck pieces of an unusual style, of which the obverse type was represented on the reverse in incuse, so that at first sight it appears as if the reverse striking has forced out the same design on the obverse. Many explanations have been given to account for this unique manner of striking. The most plausible is that when Pythagoras, the Greek philosopher and mathematician, arrived in Italy about the middle of the sixth century B.C., he soon made his influence felt in the Greek cities there and propagated his doctrine whereby every principle had its opposite, *e.g.* male and female, good and evil. The coins of these cities thus embody the doctrine, the obverse being the opposite of the reverse, the one side appearing extruded, the other 'intruded'!

Among these Italian cities was Tarentum, which through five centuries produced a fine range of silver staters, showing on the obverse its mythological founder Phalanthus on a dolphin, and on the reverse a youth and horse in many different actions, the youth sometimes seen armed and riding the horse, sometimes dismounting and sometimes leading the horse. These coins are quite common and can be purchased cheaply.

The period from about the time of the death of Alexander the Great in 323 B.C. down to Roman times is called 'Hellenistic', a name which implies that the art of the period, subject to Asiatic influences, was 'Greekish' rather than pure Greek. The coins lose their pure Greek style and tend to become rather extravagant and florid in design. Compare, for example, the tetradrachm of Mithridates the Great (120–63 B.C.), where the portrait of that ruler has been made as realistic as possible. In this period, too, the fabric of the coins tends to be flat and spread in comparison with the earlier type. What is termed the 'new style' coinage of the Athens of later days will illustrate this.

With the end of Greek independence in Roman times, no further silver coins, with certain exceptions, were struck, and the bulk of the coinage of Greece and Asia Minor under the Roman Empire is of bronze. These coins usually bear the head of the reigning emperor, with the inscription in Greek, and on the reverse a wide assortment of types having reference to gods, goddesses and monuments of the particular city. Such coins of varying sizes form a most interesting series on their own, and can provide research for the collector who is so inclined, as so many of them are unpublished in museum catalogues. They have the merit, too, of being very inexpensive.

Before leaving the subject of Greek coins of the late period, mention must be made of the coins of Alexandria in Egypt struck under the Roman Empire. These coins were struck purely for use in Egypt, which was a province subject to the Emperor's command alone, and their size and shape and metal are unique. They were struck in billon, a base silvery-coloured metal, in the first century of the Roman Empire, and were at first about the size of an ordinary tetradrachm; but later they became smaller and dumpier and their colour became a very dark brown. On the obverse appears the head of the Emperor, and on the reverse a series of religious types, embracing an amazing collection of gods of the Greek and Egyptian world. This series, too, has its rarities, but in the main these coins can be bought for a few shillings each, especially those struck in the time of the later Empire.

This chapter is only a very rough outline of the story of the Greek coinage, but we feel that sufficient has been said to prove that Greek coins are not difficult to understand and that much pleasure can be gained from a quite modest outlay.

Plate 5 ROMAN COINS

27. Denarius of Domitian.
28. Quinarius of Marcus Aurelius.
29. Sestertius of Nero.
30. Dupondius of Antoninus Pius.
31. As of Severus Alexander.
32. Antoninianus of Gordian III.

27

28

29

30

31

32

Plate 6

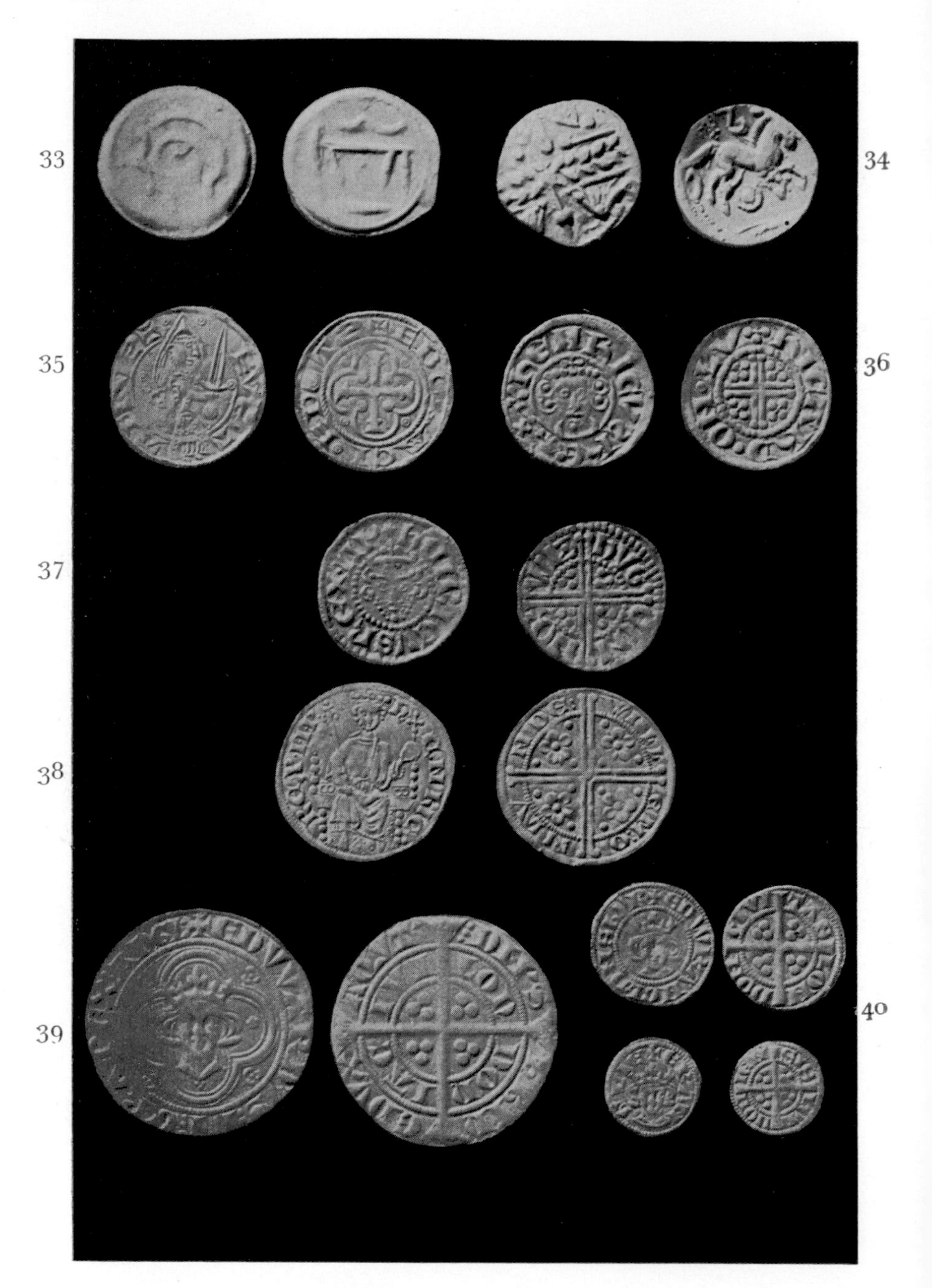

CHAPTER FIVE

Roman Coins

ROMAN coins have an undeniable fascination for many intending collectors, especially those who live in Britain. For even if their ancient history is a little shaky, they will remember reading of the expedition to Britain in 55 B.C. by the famous Roman dictator, Julius Cæsar, and realise the link with Rome that England has. Even now it is quite common to find there Roman coins of the later Empire, when the country formed an important part of the Roman world. A collector has every inclination to study the coins of Rome when he considers that the coins he acquires may have been handled by a remote ancestor of himself, who breathed the same air—perhaps a little clearer then—and suffered under the same invigorating climate as the collector himself.

With all their inclinations, so to speak, urging them to begin the collection of Roman coins, many people are held back by

Plate 6 ENGLISH COINS: ANCIENT BRITAIN TO EDWARD I

33. A so-called 'tin' coin of Ancient Britain, actually made of speculum. *Circa* 100–75 B.C.
34. An Ancient British gold Stater.
35. One of the baronial coins issued in the reign of Stephen (A.D. 1135–1154). Issued by Eustace FitzJohn (Silver).
36. Short-cross Penny (Silver).
37. Long-cross Penny, an early attempt to prevent clipping and to provide for the piece to be cut into halves and quarters (Silver).
38. Gold Penny of A.D. 1275.
39. The Groat or 'Great Piece' of Edward I (1272–1307) (Silver).
40. Silver Halfpenny and Farthing of Edward I.

their mind, which tells them that they know little of ancient history or the Latin language, and that the study of Roman coins presents difficult problems which still exercise the ingenuity of scholarly numismatists. It is quite true that the Roman series is complicated, but just as one need not have a very great depth of inquiring knowledge to appreciate the beauty and excitement of a modern jet plane at full speed, so a very elementary knowledge of Roman coins will open the gateway to a great deal of pleasure from their collection. As in the Greek series, the inscriptions of Roman coins are basically simple, especially those on coins of Imperial times, where the obverse usually bears the name and portrait of the Emperor, and the reverse some religious or political type, with an explanatory legend. Sufficient history for a reasonably full appreciation of the conditions of the times in which the coins were issued can easily be acquired, as advised in the chapter on Greek coins, from any of the numerous and well-written histories designed for the use of schools.

No collector, then, should be deterred on the grounds of the difficulty of the Roman series, and it only remains to consider the question of expense. Naturally, in every field of coin collecting there are rarities, but it is true to say that a very representative collection of Roman silver and copper coins can be built up at the cost of but a few shillings for each coin. Reference to dealers' lists will prove how really inexpensive Roman coins are, considering their great age. The reason is, of course, that the later Republic, and much more so the Empire of Rome, embraced such an extent of countries and peoples that enormous quantities of coinage were necessary.

It is usual when treating of Roman coins to make a division and deal separately with coins issued under the Roman Republic and with coins issued under the Roman Empire, which is usually considered to begin in 29 B.C. when Octavian (later to take the title of 'Augustus' and to be known as Rome's first Emperor) returned to Rome after defeating Mark Antony at the battle of Actium in 31 B.C. The coinage of the two periods is quite distinct, though the coinage of the end of the Republic points the way to its development under the Empire.

COINAGE OF THE ROMAN REPUBLIC

As far back as the fifth century B.C. bronze was used as coinage in Central Italy. It was, presumably, at first in the form of lumps of metal which changed hands according to weight. Later these developed into the form of bars and bricks of metal of a fixed weight, though the weight standards varied with the locality. At last bronze was cast in the form of a circular piece of metal with a distinctive type indicating the denomination on each side; this, then, was the first true coinage. Rome, of course, had her own particular form of this coinage, which is known as *aes grave*, or literally, 'heavy bronze': bronze struck at a definite weight. The unit of reckoning was the pound, divided into twelve ounces, as follows:

As=1 pound, mark of value, I
Semi=½ pound, mark of value S (for Semis)
Quincunx=5 ounces, mark of value . . . . .
Tremis=4 ounces, mark of value . . . .
Quadrans=3 ounces, mark of value . . .
Sextans=2 ounces, mark of value . .
Uncia (ounce)=1 ounce, mark of value .

While Rome remained a central Italian state merely, this coinage was sufficient for her internal requirements, but when she began to conquer one of her neighbours after another and to come into contact with the Greek cities of Italy, she found the clumsy aes grave unsuited to her needs and had to devise a silver coinage which would be acceptable by these cities and also by the states of Central Italy which she had overcome. For this purpose over several decades she developed a series of silver coins of varying types, which bear on the reverse the inscription 'ROMA' or 'ROMANO' (*i.e.* 'Romanorum' or of the Romans). These coins also bore a definite relationship to the aes grave, complicated by the many changes in the weights of both issues, due to the widely differing exchange value of bronze to silver in the various parts of Italy. Thus in theory the coinage of Rome was acceptable throughout Italy: the silver issues in the Greek cities and the bronze in the Italian states, and yet both were linked together in the monetary system.

The aes grave is not usually of interest to the collector, its size making it difficult to house in a normal cabinet, and further, examples in a good state of preservation are quite expensive. The silver coins can usually be obtained not too expensively and form a very pleasing addition to a collection.

With the rise of Rome a position was reached where, so far from having to accommodate her coinage to suit her neighbours she could break with past coinage and inaugurate an entirely new monetary system which Italy was bound to accept.

This system comprised three denominations of silver – the denarius (at first equal to 10 struck bronze asses of much lesser weight than the old cast aes grave, and later to 16 asses), the quinarius (or half-denarius), and the sestertius (or quarter-denarius) – and seven denominations of struck bronze (as down to semuncia or half-ounce). Apart from an unusual issue of rare gold coins, struck from gold acquired partly through war and through tribute, the above denominations represent the basic monetary system of the Roman Republic from 187 B.C. down to the civil wars of the last fifty years or so of the Republic.

At first the types of the denarius, which is by far the most common of Republican coins, were simple. The obverse bears a personification of Roma as a goddess; on the reverse is the inscription 'ROMA', below the twin patron gods of Rome, the Dioscuri, riding side by side on horseback.

The issue of coins for the Republic was controlled by a board of officials, the *Tresviri auro argento aere flando et feriundo*, or 'The three men concerned with the casting and striking of gold, silver and bronze', to give them their full title. These officials were relatively unimportant among Roman officials, and occupied the lowest rungs on the *cursus honorum*, the 'ladder of office', up every step of which an ambitious man had to pass before reaching the position of highest office, the consulship. At first these officials are unknown, as their names do not appear on the coins, but later it became the custom for one official at least, probably the chairman of the board of three, and sometimes two, to have their names incorporated in the designs of the coins struck during their term of office, which was for one year only, as were most official positions in the Roman Republic.

Shortly after these moneyers were allowed, or perhaps compelled (for they were fully responsible for the quality of the metal contained in the coins and for their correct weight), to place their names on the coins, the reverse type of the Dioscuri began to be replaced by other types, *e.g.* Victory in biga, and Jupiter in quadriga. Later still the reverse type had some reference to the moneyer's ancestors, mythical or factual, *e.g.* the denarius of the moneyer Sextus Pompeius Fostius (*circa* 130 B.C.), whose reverse shows the famous scene of the wolf suckling the twin founders of Rome, Romulus and Remus, while in the background stands the shepherd Faustulus, who in the myth found them, and from whom this Sextus Pompeius claimed his ancestry. This is a relatively simple reverse type, and many others require a Sherlock Holmes turn of mind to establish the connection between the reverse type and the moneyer. The collector will find this aspect of the coinage particularly enthralling, and there still remains a great deal for further speculation.

The obverse type of the denarius, also, does not always represent Roma, but other gods and goddesses – Mars, Jupiter, Juno, etc., etc.,—and sometimes even portrays an ancestor of the moneyer.

The other two silver coins, the quinarius and sestertius, are much rarer than the denarius. They have little interest for any but the student collector and, generally speaking, differ only from the standard silver coin, the denarius, in being proportionately smaller.

The same remarks apply to the bronze coins of the later Republic, which, moreover, are not usually found in good condition. Such coins of low value were, of course, never hoarded in ancient times and circulated till well worn.

COINAGE OF THE ROMAN EMPIRE

In the last years of the Roman Republic, in the period of the civil wars and the bitter struggle for control of Rome, it had become the custom for the various contestants to place their portraits on the coins which they themselves had struck for their respective armies. There is a series of coins bearing the heads of the famous names of the period – Cæsar, Brutus, Pompey, Mark Antony and, of course, Octavian, who later took the name of Augustus and became the first Roman Emperor. This precedent Augustus followed and maintained (as did every Roman Emperor after him) when he completely reformed the monetary system on his return to Rome a few years before the beginning of the Christian era. He began to strike regularly in gold, which had been struck only experimentally under the Republic, and his issue took the form of *aurei* (lit. 'gold coins'), in size about the same as a denarius. He continued to strike denarii and quinarii, but struck the sestertius in brass instead of silver and introduced other denominations, as the following table shows:

1 aureus=25 denarii
1 quinarius aureus (or ½ aureus)=12½ denarii
1 denarius=4 brass sestertii
1 quinarius (silver)=2 brass sestertii
1 sestertius=4 copper asses—2 brass dupondii
1 dupondius=2 copper asses
1 as=4 copper quadrantes (or ¼ asses)

It must be explained that the dupondius was almost the same size as the as. The distinguishing feature now is that the radiate head of the Emperor usually appears on the dupondius, while his head on the as is invariably laureate. They were, of course, struck in different metals, and at the time of issue must have been easily distinguishable from one another in colour.

This system of Augustus was maintained with minor changes for more than two centuries, and it was not until the time of the Emperor Caracalla (A.D. 211–217) that a new denomination, the antoninianus, named after him (his name was Antoninus), was introduced. This was a silver coin rather larger than the denarius, and distinguished from it by the radiate head of the emperor on the obverse. It is generally considered to have been worth two denarii. From Caracalla's time onwards the denarius gives place to the antoninianus as the most common Roman coin, and eventually it fades out altogether. In later and sterner times the antoninianus ceased to be made of silver and was struck in bronze, coated with a paste containing but a small amount of silver, which has entirely disappeared from the majority of such coins which have come down to us.

The above remarks represent a simplification of the Roman monetary system over the first three centuries A.D., and it must be remembered that many emperors made changes and that not every emperor struck every denomination.

Generally speaking, the Emperor had under his own charge the striking of the two important metals, gold and silver, and left the striking of baser metals, brass and copper, to the nominal government, the Senate. By virtue of this fact, the sestertius, dupondius and as, etc., while bearing the Emperor's portrait on the obverse, have somewhere in the inscription on the reverse the letters SC, standing for Senatus consulto (by decree of the Senate).

All imperial coins, except very small copper denominations, bear on the obverse the head of the Emperor, with his name and list of titles, among which figure the number of times he has held the office of tribune and consul, denoted by TR P (*tribunicia potestas*) and COS (consul), followed by Roman numerals. The series of reverse types is vast and can only be briefly mentioned here. Practically every god and goddess and personification of qualities (such as the frequent VIRTVS MILITVM, 'the courage of the soldiers') appear on the coins. The sestertii of the early Empire, being the largest coins, lend themselves particularly well to the ambitious die engraver. On the coins of Trajan (A.D. 98–117), for example, his public buildings are beautifully depicted, while on those of Hadrian (A.D. 117–138) the Emperor's visits to the various provinces are recalled by types showing the Emperor being greeted by personifications of the provinces. Hence sestertii in a good state of preservation and well patinated by the action of the soil are much sought after by collectors, and frequently realise a price in excess of an aureus of the same ruler. An irony indeed, when one recalls that an aureus in Roman times was worth one hundred sestertii!

It is a wise and proper course for the beginner to decide from the outset which denomination and metal he will collect. Very few people can afford to collect aurei alone, but the majority of collectors can afford denarii and antoniniani, and can obtain a nice selection showing the portraits of the majority of the Roman emperors for but a small outlay – with perhaps an aureus here and there!

A collection of sestertii, as hinted above, may prove expensive, but these coins represent good value for the money and will always be admired.

The series of asses and dupondii has been much neglected, but a collection of these smaller coins will prove little inferior as a source of enjoyment to the collector and will certainly cost much less.

Whatever denomination the beginner decides upon, he need have no fear that he will ever regret having begun to collect Roman coins. He will find that the fascination and enjoyment grow with every fresh coin he acquires, and in proportion as his knowledge increases.

Plate 7 ENGLISH COINS: EDWARD III to HENRY VIII

41. The original English Florin, gold piece issued by Edward III (1327–77).
42. The gold Noble of Edward III, with the famous obverse design showing the king standing in a ship.
43. A gold Anglo-Gallic coin, the Salute of St. Lô, issued by Henry VI (1422–61/71). The obverse of the piece, issued in the period 1470–71 after the restoration of Henry VI, shows on this side an angel saluting the Virgin. Between them is a scroll inscribed AVE, while the shields of the arms of France and England are seen at the base of the figures.
44. A Half-Groat (twopence) of Henry VIII (1509–47). Note on the reverse the letters T W on either side of the shield. These were for Thomas Wolsey, and his cardinal's hat is seen below the shield of arms.

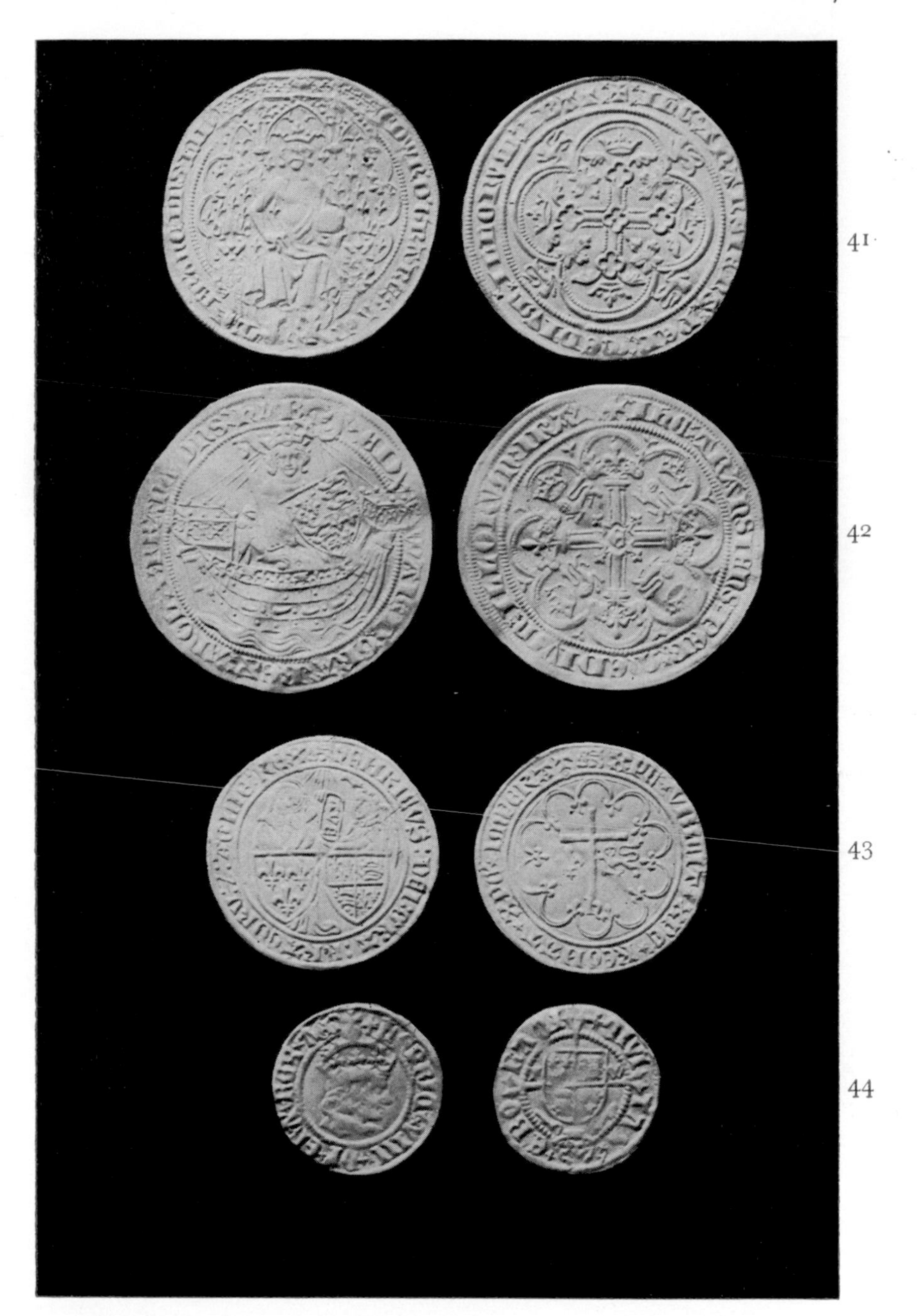
41
42
43
44

45

46

47

CHAPTER SIX

The Coinage of England

I. ITS EARLY DEVELOPMENT

IT IS A fortunate circumstance for collectors that the English series falls into two quite distinct sections, the hammered coins and the milled. There are a great many collectors who specialise in one of these two sections. Each is subdivided into smaller parts, usually at the will of the individual. Some idea of the various sections into which a collection may fall can be formed as a description of the English series proceeds.

Some passing mention has already been made of the coins which were in use in Britain during the Roman occupation. Though actually belonging to the Roman series, there are many collectors who feel that the English series cannot be regarded as complete without the inclusion of such of the Roman issues as were in use in this country during the occupation.

But the Romans did not introduce coinage into the country. The first coins which were current were, as far as can be established, a series of gold coins whose design was based on the

Plate 8 ENGLISH COINS: EDWARD THE BLACK PRINCE, HENRY VIII, EDWARD VI

45. Gold 'Pavilion' or Royal d'Or of Bordeaux, of Edward the Black Prince (1330–76). The Prince is seen standing beneath a Gothic portico. One of the fine pieces of the Anglo-Gallic series.
46. Gold Double Sovereign of Henry VIII (1509–47), showing the king enthroned. Note the portcullis at his feet, adopted as the badge of the Tudors.
47. Silver Crown of Edward VI (1547–53), dated 1551. The young king is shown on horseback. Though figures had been shown on horseback before this time the detailed workmanship of this early attempt at animated figures is worthy of note.

gold staters of Philip II of Macedon. This coinage arrived from Gaul with the Belgic invaders, and before its advent various currency bars of iron of a more or less fixed weight served the purpose of coins. A parallel can be drawn here with the obols of Ancient Greece.

According to the evidence of finds most of the early coins were mainly in circulation in the southern parts of Britain, or in such parts as were easy of access from the mainland of Europe. It has been recognised that in ancient times it was a far simpler matter to sail to England from Europe than to journey overland from the south of this country to the north. Overseas contacts must, therefore, have been far stronger than those with the hinterland.

This early coinage has come to be referred to as Bellovacian, from its origin, and consisted mainly of staters and quarter-staters. Its period is from about 100 to 75 B.C.

At about the same period what has come to be known as the Early British tin money was in circulation. This is considered to be the first native coinage of Britain. The coins were cast, generally in wooden moulds and in strips, from which they were broken apart, and their design was crude in the extreme. A very rough head, believed to represent that of Apollo, occupied one side. A crude representation of a bull filled the reverse. The coins were not actually pure tin, at this period one of the staple exports, but were made of a metal which has been named speculum. It consisted of a proportion of 22·1 per cent tin, 4·6 per cent lead, 72·4 per cent copper and 0·4 per cent iron. The moulds in which the coins were cast were of wood. Its grain can sometimes be seen on the actual pieces, and when new the coins were bright and shiny in appearance, akin to silver. Hence the name assigned to the metal. When found today they are mostly corroded and dull in appearance. They have come to light in various places in the south of the country, one of the latest finds being at Sunbury, in Middlesex.

The Ancient British series continues, their types being strongly influenced by the first Belgic Invasion. Again the obverse type consists of portions of a laureate head of Apollo, now degenerating in type, while the reverse shows a crude form of disjointed horse. It is composed mainly of a number of simple lines and dots. In some types the obverse was plain. Gold coins, staters, make their appearance *circa* 75–55 B.C. These again resemble the early coins brought over by the Belgic invaders, and again they are found mainly in the south of the country. Subdivisions, quarter-staters, are also found.

The various tribes which ruled sections of the country issued their own crude coins, some with local rulers' names on them. Thus we get coins of the Regni and Atrebates occurring in Berkshire, Hampshire, Surrey and Sussex. Coins of the Trinovantes are found in Essex and Suffolk, those of the Catuvellauni in Buckinghamshire, Bedfordshire, Cambridge, Essex, Hertfordshire, Hampshire, Northamptonshire, Oxfordshire and Suffolk, those of the Cantii in Kent, the Dobuni in Gloucestershire, Herefordshire, Monmouthshire, Oxfordshire, Somersetshire, Wiltshire and Worcestershire, those of the Iceni in Cambridge, Norfolk and Suffolk, the Brigantes in Yorkshire and North Lincolnshire, and those of the Cortinani or South Brigantes in South Lincolnshire, Leicestershire and Northamptonshire.

These coins occupy the period around the time of the invasion of the country by the Romans, first under Julius Cæsar. The gradual conquest of the country saw the increase of the dominance of Roman coins, which ultimately ousted the local types. Eventually, Roman coins were actually struck in Britain, and the phase ends with the British imitations of the Roman type. This brings us in time to the period of the third and fourth centuries.

From the Roman types and copies of them there gradually emerged the Anglo-Saxon types, which were established by use about the fifth century A.D. For about a century the sceat, a small, crude copper piece, was in use. Many of the coins bear a head or portions thereof, and some of the legends are in Runic script.

By about the middle of the sixth century local types, which can be traced to definite issuers, again emerged. Notable among these are the coins struck by the Kings of Northumbria and Kent and the Archbishops of York. Again the types are crude, some still showing strong Roman influence; some more religious types, the cross making its appearance in various forms.

By about the end of the seventh century A.D. a definite type had begun to emerge, which was to hold the field for some four hundred years. This was the silver penny, a thin disc of metal, something larger than the farthing, and with various devices shown on it.

In its early stages this type of coin was issued by the Kings of Kent, Mercia, East Anglia, Wessex, the Archbishops of Canterbury and the Viking invaders.

Most of these coins of the early Anglo-Saxon period are rare, and many famous names which have come down to us through history are associated with them. There are coins of Burgred and Æthelstan; those of St. Edmund; memorials to the Danish settlers; those of Cnut (*circa* 890) and of Æthelred I (866–871).

In about the middle of the tenth century more determined and persistent attempts at portraits began to establish themselves, and heads and busts appear frequently. Though they can bear little resemblance to the person they attempted to portray, they are of considerable historic interest.

The period of the coins of the kings of all England begins with Edgar (959–975). It will be remembered that this monarch

Plate 9 ENGLISH COINS: MARY TUDOR, ELIZABETH I

48. Gold Sovereign of Mary Tudor (1553–58), issued in the period 1553–54, before her marriage to Philip of Spain.
49. Silver Crown of Elizabeth I (1558–1603). The mint-mark 1, on both sides, dates the piece as 1601.
50. The silver 'Portcullis Crown' of Elizabeth I, issued in 1600 (mint-mark o). Issued to support trading with the East, these 'portcullis' dollars were equal to 8 Spanish Reales, and were our first 'Empire' coins. They were issued by the English East India Company, who in later times provided the early 'Empire' coins for overseas trading.

48
49
50

51

52

is mainly famous for his relatively pacific reign, his increase of the fleet, which circumnavigated the country once a year on a patrol which was to have much to do with the absence of Danish invasions, his meeting with six kings at Chester in 973 when they pledged their allegiance to him, and his coronation at Bath in 973, fifteen years after his proclamation and accession.

Until now the obverse legends on the silver pennies had, in the main, consisted of the monarch's name, with the name of the moneyer appearing on the reverse. From about 975 (Edward the Martyr) we begin to find the addition of the name of the mint in the reverse legend, and to many collectors this adds a considerable interest to the issues, since it gives a very strong local interest to the coins. Moreover, coin striking had gradually improved, and the lettering had become progressively easier to read to modern eyes. The names of the towns are often abbreviated, and the spelling differs from that of our own time – as Wihrac for Worcester; Eboracm and others similar for York – but a little study of the coins soon familiarises the student with these differences, and numerous lists of the names rendered into modern form exist.

Plate 10 ENGLISH COINS: JAMES I

51. Gold Sovereign of James I (1603–25).
52. Silver Crown of James I. Though James was a nervous type who hated strife, he delighted to be shown on horseback, sword on shoulder, or in the guise of a Roman Emperor, as on his coronation medal and Laurel pieces.

This system of placing the name of the moneyer and the mint on the coins continues over the period of the Norman Invasion, and at its height something like one hundred mints can be traced by their issues. Indeed, practically every town of importance was striking coins.

The cross, or a cruciform design, continues to dominate the field on the reverse, and the word PAX, spelt either PAXS or PAX, sometimes appears. During the civil wars of Stephen there are a number of irregular and rare baronial issues, while the coins themselves reflect by their rough workmanship and shape the unrest of the times.

An interesting series of coins appears with the reign of Henry II (1154–89). Basically the design of the silver pennies as a whole differs little, but in 1180 what are known as the Short Cross coins appeared. These continued to be issued till 1247, and retained on the obverse the name HENRICVS throughout the period. No English coins are known with the names of Richard I (1189–99) or John (1199–1216). The issue continues till 1247, well into the reign of Henry III (1216-72), and during the period many local mints and moneyers were in operation, though not so many as in the period Æthelred II to William II. On the reverse the legend consists of the moneyer's name and the name of the mint, as ADAM ON LVN (Adam at London), and the centre of the field is occupied by a grooved cross. This was made up of four L-shaped lines with ornaments in the angles. This series, which various authorities have grouped and assigned to the period of the kings concerned, forms probably the best as well as one of the least expensive of the silver penny series for those having an interest in local townships.

The design of these coins was no defence against the prevalent evil of clipping. So bad did this evil become that, in 1247, a Council was convened at Oxford to consider the whole matter. Its recommendations that the standard of the coin should be changed was set aside, and the form of the coin itself was altered. The cross was now made to play a defensive rôle. The new coins had the cross extended to the edges, for which reason they are known as the Long Cross type. Any pennies on which the four ends of the cross were not visible were in future to be declared illegal. For the first time also the numeral was added to the king's name, HENRICVS REX TERCIUS, later HENRICVS REX III. The whole of the coinage at the royal mints was leased to the king's brother, the Earl of Cornwall, and the amount of coin replacement rendered necessary by the change kept a number of mints busy.

In cases where numbers of these local mints were in operation, it should not be assumed that they were all at work either at one time or throughout the reign. Coin is supplied to meet demand, and many of the mints in smaller towns came into operation only as required, sometimes for only short periods.

As will have been noted, during the long period of time, some five hundred years, in which the penny had been the main coin of the realm, no mention has been made of any gold coinage. In 1275, however, an attempt was made to establish a gold currency by the striking of a pure gold penny. This piece was made current at twenty pence. This followed the issue of a gold florin in Italy, a piece which took its name from Florence, where it was struck. The gold penny failed to become popular, probably because it was valued at below the market price of gold. No doubt it was sold for its bullion value. Later its valuation in currency rose to twenty-four pence, but the coin still failed to obtain public confidence. Though there is no record of its being officially withdrawn, it is not likely to have remained in currency for long. Very few specimens of this fine example of mediæval coiners' art remain in existence, and these coins are now of great rarity.

This apparent official mistake of issuing a coin to be current at less than its metal value is not an isolated example. It occurs again, as we shall presently see.

But there must have been something of a need for the issue of a denomination larger than the penny, and in the reign of Edward I (1272–1307) we find the first appearance of the groat, or great piece, current at the value of four pence. This coin was ordered in 1279, but again the period of circulation of the piece seems to have been a short one, and the coin itself is a rarity today. Halfpennies and farthings were also coined with the new coinage of 1279, and these obviated the necessity of cutting the pennies into halves and quarters for the same purpose. This practice had also given plenty of opportunity for clipping.

A word should be said here about the pennies, still the staple coin, of Edward I, Edward II and Edward III. These coins, different in appearance in many respects from the long and short cross coins which preceded them, are difficult to allocate to their respective reigns. It will have been deduced from the dates given above that the coins of Henry III continued to circulate well into the reign of Edward I, whose coins did not begin to appear in his own name till seven years after his accession. This long gap may well have been due to the fact that the coinage was still in a poor state from the economic point of view, and clipping was still a considerable evil. To attempt to solve the various coinage problems the Council had been deliberating for many years, and it was not until 1279 that their deliberations matured in the form of the new coinage, with its additional denominations. The type of penny now introduced was carried on into the next two reigns without the addition of a numeral after the king's name. In this way the allocation difficulty arises for the collector.

Though only pennies, halfpennies and farthings were struck during the reign of Edward II (1307–27), in the reign of Edward III (1327–77) gold coins again made their appearance. The first of these was the gold florin, proclaimed in January 1344. Its value was six shillings, but on account of the high value at which it was rated in proportion to silver, the coin was so unpopular that it was withdrawn in the following August. Half- and quarter-florins were also coined, and owing to their hasty recall all are now of the very highest rarity.

Throughout the history of the gold coinage the fineness of the metal has been varied from time to time, and this fineness is computed upon the 'carat pound'. The pound is divided into 24 parts, called carats, and each carat is again divided into quarters, called grains. Pure gold is therefore of 24 carats, and is too soft to stand much wear. Alloying is carried out primarily to increase the durability of the metal, the florins of Edward III being 23 carats, 3½ grains of pure gold with ½ grain of alloy.

2. A BIMETALLIC COINAGE ESTABLISHED

In spite of the failure of the gold florin, there was a definite need for a gold currency. This was met in August 1344 by the issue of a gold noble, value 6*s*. 8*d*. This name for the coin is supposed to have been derived from the noble nature of the metal, gold having always been regarded as regal. This fine coin, of which halves and quarters eventually appeared, showed the king standing in a ship, and this may have been suggested by the naval victory of Sluys in 1340.

As a general rule, from this time forward the legend on the coins of England detailed the various lands over which the king or queen of the period ruled, actually or nominally, apart from England itself. Some of these territorial claims continued to appear on coins long after the actual territory had been relinquished. As an example, the title to the sovereignty of France continues to appear till the reign of George III. Henry II (1154–89) was the first English monarch to strike money for the French domains, thus starting a series of coins now known as Anglo-Gallic. The titles to overseas domains began to appear on English coins in the reign of Edward III, and the issues of the reign show three examples of such titles. The coins of the period 1351–61 show Edward styled King of France but not Lord of Aquitaine; those from 1361–69 style him Lord of Aquitaine but omit the French title, under one of the terms of the Treaty of Brétigny (May 8, 1360); then those from 1369–77 credit him with both titles, the Treaty having been broken. Some credit him with four titles, England, France, Ireland and Aquitaine.

The changing titles shown on the legends of coins reflect to some extent the changing fortunes of the country concerned; though the continued use of titles to which the country no longer had a right, or the assumption of titles to which the ruler was not entitled, often coupled with the use of any appropriate arms, has led to more than one international incident. This applies equally to English coinage, the title to France and the French arms, three lilies or fleur-de-lis, being retained till 1800, though the King of England had not been entitled to them for some centuries, Calais, the last French possession, being lost in 1558. Within our own times, IND. IMP. (Emperor of India) has been dropped from British coinage, promptly upon the former Indian Empire attaining self-government. The deliberations upon the subject of the correct titles of Queen Elizabeth II are still fresh in the minds of many.

Gold nobles, half-nobles and quarter-nobles, and silver groats, half-groats, pennies, halfpennies and farthings, continue to be the staple denominations in use through the reigns of Edward III, Richard II (1377–99), Henry IV (1399–1413) and Henry V (1413–22), with the angel and half-angel appearing in the reign of Henry VI. In the reign of Edward IV (1461–83) the rose-noble, with its halves and quarters, was added, the coin being so called on account of the rose which was stamped on both sides. This flower was one of the badges of the king. The sun was another, but though it was used as a mint mark at various periods, no 'sun nobles' ever appeared.

The study of mint marks, or privy marks as some of them are called, is an important part of the study of coinage. A list of English mint marks is given in the Appendix. They occur in various places on a coin, but in the English series they often appear at the beginning of the legend on the obverse and/or the reverse.

Mint marks consist of some small device or badge, generally having reference to the monarch, such as the sun mentioned above, a portcullis or a rose. They can also refer to the town in which the particular mint issuing the coin is situated, in which case they are often the initial letter of the place, such as B for Bristol, C for Coventry or later Chester, E for York (Eboracum) or later for Edinburgh. Their purpose is varied, but mainly they indicate either the date of minting, the place of minting, the monarch or noble who issued the coin, or the place from which the metal for the coin came.

It is hardly to be expected that the reign of the uncrowned Edward V, who only reigned from April 9 to June 22, 1483, would be marked by the issue of any coinage. Some does, however, exist, angels and half-angels, groats, pennies and halfpennies, being attributed to him. They can only be identified from the coins of the previous reign, by their mint marks, a rose and sun united, or a boar's head. The latter was the badge of the Protector, later Richard III, who is generally credited with the murder of Edward V and his brother, the young Duke of York – the controversial 'Princes in the Tower' mystery. In the seventeenth century remains, believed to be these of the two children, were found, buried under the stone floor within the confines of that gloomy fortress, in a spot now pointed out to the many visitors to the Tower of London.

The short reign of the 'wicked uncle', Richard III (1483–85), was marked numismatically only by the issue of angels and half-angels, groats, half-groats and pennies. Various provincial mints were in operation over the whole of this period of history, and even the relatively small coinage of Richard III has issues from the Tower, York and Durham. The pennies from the last two mints were issued by Archbishop Rotherham (1480–1500) and Bishop John Sherwood (1483–94), respectively. This demonstrates how, during the whole of this period, certain smaller denominations were issued by various ecclesiastical dignitaries or by the great Lords. The issue of certain coins by Cardinal Wolsey, with his Cardinal's hat by way of privy mark, was to be one of the causes of his fall, in the reign of Henry VIII, which we are now fast approaching.

The reign of Henry VII (1485–1509) saw some expansion in the coinage, ryals or nobles, sovereigns, angels and half-angels being issued, the silver coins consisting of the shilling, groat, half-groat, penny, halfpenny and farthings.

It will be noted that two new denominations, the names of which have lasted till our own times, have now appeared, the sovereign and the shilling. The first, a very handsome gold coin, showing the king enthroned, a very elaborate design, was first coined in 1489. It was twice the weight of the ryal or noble, sometimes considered in this reign as a half-sovereign, and was current for 20*s*.

The shilling appeared in 1504, and has been considered by some to have been only a trial issue. It was current at 12*d*., as now, and was at first called a testoon.

Two other points of general interest occur in this reign. We now have the first instance, apart from certain coins in the reign of Henry III, in which the numeral occurs after the king's name, another custom which was to be carried on into our own time. The second point: for the first time we now have a genuine portrait of the king, executed with considerable skill, appearing on the coinage. This custom, starting with the shilling and the groat, and gradually in succeeding reigns spreading over the whole of the denominations, gives an added interest to coin collecting.

Before proceeding to the coins of the reign of Henry VIII, a reign almost as famous numismatically as in so many other ways, a word should be said about a series of coins mentioned earlier in this section, the Anglo-Gallic issues.

This series of coins is generally considered as a sub-section of the English series, and is one in which a number of collectors have at various times specialised exclusively. It begins, as stated above, in the reign of Henry II and continues on till Henry VI (1422–61, restored 1470–71). Here the series ends apart from a few groats struck by Henry VIII, when the series finally closes, Calais being lost to England in the next reign but one.

One of the most interesting sections of this series is that of the coinage of Edward the Black Prince (1330–76). His father, Edward III, granted to him the Duchy of Aquitaine in 1362, when it was created a principality. The Black Prince had mints at Agen, Bordeaux, Fontenoy or Frigeac, La Rochelle or La Réole, Limoges or Lectoure, Poitiers and Tarbes, from which coins with the colourful names of Leopards, Royal d'Or of Bordeaux, also called Pavilions, and other unusual names appeared.

Names such as Leopard and Pavilion bore direct reference to the devices to be found on the coins, and throughout our numismatic history this habit of calling coins by popular names based upon their appearance constantly recurs. Reference has been made to the noble, and the student will find such names as Laurel, Rider, Bonnet Piece, Lion, Angel, Guinea and Sovereign occurring in the English and Scottish series. Indeed the custom spreads far outside the confines of Britain, and some reference to these names will occur here and there in the course of this review of coinage.

While mentioning Anglo-Gallic coins, some reference should also be made to a similar series which occurs with the accession of the House of Hanover (George I) to the throne of England.

Anglo-Hanoverian coins were then issued, a series which continued till the reign of Queen Victoria, upon whose accession it ceased. This series is, however, generally considered to belong to the study of continental coins, though at least one writer has included it under English colonial issues.

The reign of Henry VIII (1509–47) is a notable one for many events, most of which are fairly well known to those who possess no particular knowledge of history. In the numismatic field the reign is noteworthy on account of a considerable variety of coins, issued in various series, and in particular for the gradual debasement of the coinage which these numerous issues marked.

The various series or issues of coins during a reign have not so far been explained. When it is necessary for any reason to change the style or type or fineness of a coin or coins, the new pieces have to be proclaimed by the Sovereign and approved by the Sovereign and Parliament. We have already seen the issue of the first coinage of Queen Elizabeth II. If it were necessary to change the design of these coins, if a new denomination such as a four-shilling piece were to be issued, or now it is decided to alter the whole system of the coinage and base it on the decimal system, the new coin or coins which appear will be the second issue of the reign.

Thus, in the reign of Henry VIII we have a series of coins which have been classified into five different issues. Broadly speaking, each saw a downward trend in the intrinsic value of the coinage. The first coinage of the reign lasted from 1509 till 1526. It marks the period during which Henry was squandering the enormous wealth that his father had accumulated.

As in previous reigns, the evils of clipping and counterfeiting continued on a considerable scale, and the importation of French and Flemish gold coins, a dangerous evil over many reigns, continued in a manner sufficient to endanger the coinage and thus the economic life of the country.

In 1526 steps were taken, in part to remedy some of these evils. In the event they were to prove disastrous. A new issue of coins, the second (1526–43), was made. Gold coinage was gradually debased till it reached 22 carat, and the older or first issue gold coins were reduced in weight to conform to the new standard of value. This debasement went on through the third issue (1543), the fourth issue (1544), the fifth issue (1545), and the final result was that by the end of the reign not only had gold been reduced to 20 carat, but silver coins were debased so much as to contain only one part of silver to two parts of alloy. The very frequency of the issues shows the unstable nature of the coinage and the internal economy of the country. As a result of this, the silver coins of these issues which have come down to us are often so poor as to appear almost like copper.

One or two points of interest, apart from the economic considerations, affect the coins themselves. At the beginning of the reign, though the name of the king on the coinage was changed from Henry VII to Henry VIII, or in some cases '8', such coins as were portrait coins still continued to bear the effigy of Henry VII. A clear-cut dividing line at the end of a reign had not then been established and a portrait coin was still a novelty. The continuance of the old portrait excited little comment.

At its commencement the reign was full of promise. Ample wealth permitted the issue of beautiful double sovereigns, thought to be patterns and now very rare, and sovereigns of great artistic merit were also coined. They show the king (actually Henry VII) in robes of state, crowned and with the sceptre and orb in his hands, seated on the throne with a portcullis, the special mark of Henry VII, beneath his feet. On the reverse the royal arms are enshrined in the heart of a Tudor rose.

Though similar, artistically fine coins continued to be struck in later issues, their quality began to go down as debasement proceeded. Wolsey, directed to equate the standard of the coinage to that of foreign countries in 1526, revalued the sovereign at 22*s*. as against 20*s*. before, and reduced the gold content by 1 cat. 3½ grs. to 22 cat. The new alloy was known as 'crown gold', since the coins struck from it were crowns. Though some coins still appeared in the better quality gold they were few, and the gradual reduction continued during the reign, as stated above, till 20 carat gold was reached in 1545.

Various mints were in operation besides London, including those of Canterbury, York, Durham and Bristol. The reign is also notable for the different coins issued by authorities other than the king himself. Though such coins are all of minor denominations, they bear the privy mark or mint mark of the issuer. Thus, half-groats were issued at Canterbury by Archbishop Warham (1504–32), and bear the letters WA. Half-groats were issued at York by Archbishop Bainbridge (1508–14), and have the letters XB. Coins were also issued by Cardinal Wolsey, letters T.W.; by Archbishop Cranmer and Bishop Tunstall, with letters T.C. and C.D., respectively. A cardinal's hat also appears in appropriate cases.

The constant changes and debasement of the coinage resulted in a chaos such as has probably never since been seen in England. Though the squandering of national wealth in two world wars left a gigantic problem to be faced by the administration of our day, notably by the late Sir Stafford Cripps, it is doubtful if even he was faced with quite the complexity of problems regarding the coinage which the administrators of Edward VI (1547–53) were called upon to solve.

When the boy-king Edward VI came to the throne in 1547 the coinage was in a bad state indeed. Not only was it so debased that some of the denominations were almost valueless, but coins of the same denominations but of different weights and fineness were in circulation together. The confusion can well be imagined. Though the administration of the time set about restoring the coinage to a proper fineness, it was impossible, for economic reasons, to abandon the base coinage altogether. It is paradoxical, therefore, to find the coinage history of the reign consisting of efforts to restore the coinage while, at the same time, issuing coins even more base than those of Henry VIII. Moreover, many of these poor coins came from the same mints as those of better quality. Most of the base coins issued were of small denomination. The main source of bullion for them was found in the testoons or shillings of Henry VIII, which were recoined into baser metal in order to provide revenue to meet the cost of producing the better coins.

The coinage of Edward VI falls into three periods. The first (1547–49) is of interest since some of the earlier coins bore the name of Henry VIII, while the king was shown with the features of Edward VI; and Brooke states (*English Coins*) that there 'was also a large output in other denominations without a change of either the name or the portrait'. During the second part of the first period, coins with both the effigy and title of Edward VI were issued. Coins during this period were still debased, gold being 20 carat. The second period (1549–50) saw an improvement in gold coins, the fineness being raised to 22 carat, while the third period (1550–53) saw gold raised to 23 carat.

Mints at Bristol and Southwark were in operation besides that at the Tower, and in December 1548 the former palace of the Bishops of Durham, Durham House in the Strand, about on the site of the present Adelphi, was furnished with a mint and commenced to issue coins. Though its output is said to have been considerable, it closed again, in October 1549.

One of the events of great importance to the collector of coins was the first issue, in 1551, of the silver crown. In the previous reign crowns had been issued in 'crown gold', but there was now added a handsome silver piece, showing the king on horseback, with the date below and the royal arms on the reverse. This was the commencement of the long line of silver crowns which, with the exception of the reign of Mary, has continued down to our own times, though in some cases, *i.e.* in the reign of William IV, only proofs were issued.

As previously stated, there are many collectors who specialise in crown pieces almost exclusively. The size of the coin gives ample scope for fine portraiture and good design, and there are sufficient types and varieties to make the series a most interesting one to collect. The four hundredth anniversary of the striking of the first silver crown fell in 1951, and was celebrated by the issue of the second type of crown piece coined during the reign of George VI. This was a cupro-nickel piece, and its issue also conicided with the Festival of Britain, which itself marked the centenary of the Great Exhibition of 1851. Quite a large number of crowns were struck at a special branch mint set up on the Festival site, almost opposite the one-time Durham House mint on the opposite side of the river. So much interest was aroused that, in all, some 2 m. 1951 crowns were struck, and visitors carried them to all parts of the world.

It is pleasant to recall that the crown piece issued to mark the

Coronation of Queen Elizabeth II reverted to the custom of showing the monarch on horseback, undoubtedly one of the most pleasing types of design that can be used for so fine a piece. Unfortunately, the piece was so poorly executed as to be a mockery of the type of coin which it chose to emulate. A golden opportunity to show what modern minting could produce was thus thoughtlessly cast away. This piece was also criticised by some as being too medallic in appearance to be a satisfactory coin.

Yet so great was the interest aroused by the piece that some 5 m. were struck, which once more reached all parts of the globe, partly by the hands of visitors. Though in some previous reigns, such as that of George VI, the crown appeared in company with all the other denominations issued to mark the new reign, the Coronation crown of Queen Elizabeth II was the first in the series to be issued as a definite Coronation commemorative crown. A different design was authorised for use at a later date in the reign and crowns of this type appeared in 1960. A large number were sent to New York in connection with the British Fair held there in that year.

Gold coins were, of course, issued during the reign of Edward VI. Gold crowns actually appeared during the first period (1547–49). Sovereigns, halves and quarters appeared, and a half-quarter-sovereign (2*s.* 6*d.*) was struck in gold. Though short, the reign contained great variety of numismatic material.

The reign of Mary I (1553–58) is probably almost as well known for certain of its aspects as is that of Elizabeth I. She is remembered mainly on account of her devotion to the Roman Catholic Church, whose roots in this country her father, Henry VIII, had done so much to sever. The persecution which followed in the wake of Mary's religious zeal has left an abiding mark upon history.

As with all other history, events developed slowly. When Mary came to the throne the Protestant Church was not fully established, nor was the Roman Catholic Church completely obliterated. Mary tried to reverse, with not very happy results, the trend of events which her father had started – events which were to be carried further towards their conclusion by her sister, Elizabeth I, in due time. Perhaps a parallel can be drawn with the events of our own time, when one political party undertakes the great revolution of nationalising the industries of the country, while the party which succeeds it tries to reverse the yet uncompleted programme.

From the coinage point of view Mary's reign falls into two parts – that when she reigned alone, from 1553 to 1554, and that when she and Philip of Spain shared the throne, from 1554 to 1558. It is not often remembered that among the marriage projects for this queen was one for her union with the Emperor Charles V, the father of Philip, and one for her marriage with Francis I of France, whose grandson Francis II eventually married Mary, Queen of Scots. Had the kingdoms of England and France been brought closer by such a marriage, history would undoubtedly have taken a very different course. As it was, Mary engaged in a war with France, at the instance of Philip. Far from bringing the kingdoms closer, this war resulted in the final loss of Calais, for so long an English possession and an important mint town.

The coinage itself shows no great changes from previous reigns. No sensational new denominations were issued. The main event of significance was the inclusion of the name of Philip before that of Mary on the coins issued after 1554, and the appearance on the shillings and sixpences of both busts, placed face to face.

The finest piece of the reign is undoubtedly the sovereign, value 30*s*. This is a magnificent example of the larger type of hammered gold coin, showing Mary enthroned in state. The coin, when dated, is dated in Roman figures, both for the years 1553 and 1554. The rarest coins of the first period are the half-angel and the ryal of 15*s*. Groats and halves, together with pennies, were issued before Mary's marriage. After her marriage, besides angels and half-angels, shillings and half-shillings (or sixpences), groats and halves were also struck. An issue common to both periods was a base penny, of 3 oz. fine. The gold coins of both periods were of 23 cat. 3½ grs., and the silver apart from the base pennies was 11 oz fine.

3. ELIZABETH I TO JAMES I

The period of history during which Elizabeth I reigned in England has, both by the greatness of the Queen herself and that of her heroes, so captured the imagination of the average man that little needs to be said about the main historical events. In retrospect, it was a reign in which the people of England asserted themselves; in which the country not only regained its former greatness after many years of reverses, but rose to new heights of heroic endeavour. It was an age of exploration and adventure, one which, though somewhat highly coloured in the popular imagination now, has justly gone down in history as great. Finally expelled from the mainland of Europe, the nation began to look elsewhere, mainly to the then newly discovered American continent, for space in which to expand both its population and its trade. With the final overthrow of Spain with the defeat of the Armada, 1588, the way to expansion began to open up, and the very earliest foundations of American colonial development began to take shape.

On the famous Spanish eight reales piece, two pillars had been shown as part of the reverse device. They were intended to signify the Pillars of Hercules, that is, the mouth of the Mediterranean Sea which, until the time of Columbus, had been virtually the end of the world. There had always been contrary rumours and speculation, but nothing factual was known. The motto on the coin, which may be translated as 'NOTHING BEYOND' (this), *i.e.* 'here is the end of the world', had already been rudely shaken. This legend was now finally proved false, both by the Spaniards and by English seamen with, as climax, the circumnavigation of the globe by Drake, who finally achieved that which Columbus died believing he had accomplished.

From the numismatic point of view, the reign of Elizabeth I was one of constant effort to bring back the coinage to something approaching its former standards. Interest also lies, to some extent, in the preservation of fine portraits of the Queen on her coinage, notably on the then almost new piece, the silver crown.

Early in the reign the process of gradually restoring the coinage was continued. There was still a considerable amount of the base money of Edward VI in circulation. Some of the baser classes of testoon (shilling) were countermarked with a portcullis or a greyhound and made current at 4½*d.* and 2½*d.* In 1561 they were finally demonetised, together with other base money which had gradually been derated. A separate establisment with its own Under-Treasurer was added to the mint about 1560, to cope with the work of converting the base coinage into standard silver. As a result, the countermarked pieces of Edward VI just mentioned are of considerable rarity, as most of them found their way into the melting-pot.

Rumours became current that the coinage was to be reduced in value, and although proclamations were issued which made such rumours illegal, the coinage was in fact reduced in value by one-third in 1562. Ten years later a new coinage was ordered at the old values and the process of restoring the coinage thus took another step forward.

Another point of importance was that the trials of the pyx, whereby certain coins of every minting are set aside and tested to prove that they are of the correct fineness and value, were

Plate 11 ENGLISH COINS: CHARLES I

53. The Frontispiece shows the silver Pound piece, struck at Shrewsbury during the Civil War. It is the largest English silver coin struck for circulation.
54. The silver Oxford Crown of Charles I (1625–49). Note the view of the town of Oxford below the horse.
55. Civil War Half-crown of Charles I. The mint-mark of three pears, the arms of Worcestershire, indicate that the piece was struck in that county, probably at Hartlebury Castle.
56. Civil War Half-crown of the Parliamentary forces. Though still showing Charles on horseback, the mint mark (P) indicates that the piece was struck by the Parliamentary party, who held the London mint at the Tower.

RELIG·PROT·LEG
ANG·LIBER·PARL
1644
OXON
54
55
56

57
CR
OBS
1648
58
CR
V S
59
THE COMMONWEALTH OF ENGLAND
GOD WITH VS 1652
V

ordered to be restored to three-monthly periods, having been made annual by Edward VI. Records, however, show the pyx trials to have been almost always an annual event, but one sees in the Order an attempt towards restoring public confidence in the coin of the realm.

New silver denominations appeared, of sixpence (instead of half-testoon or half-shilling), threepence, three-halfpence and three-farthings. It was also ordered that 10 lb. weight of pennies should be set aside each year for the Queen's own use. It is thought that these may have been used for the annual ceremony of the Maundy distribution, of which more will be said at a later stage, for the purpose of largesse.

The introduction of the two very minor denominations just instanced probably reflects the need for a series of small denominations, to fill which gap tokens appeared. A copper coinage was considered but this did not materialise for some time to come, and the tokens, which were of lead and tin, were issued by traders of the time to supply the need. How great a significance such tokens were to assume will be dealt with when considering the coinages of a later reign.

Some patterns were struck for halfpence and farthings in

Plate 12 ENGLISH COINS: SIEGE PIECES AND COMMONWEALTH

57. Civil War siege piece of 1648, struck at Pontefract Castle, which is shown on the reverse. Made by stamping a piece of silver, roughly cut from household silver articles. Such pieces sometimes contain the hall-mark of the original article of plate.
58. Ormonde Money. A silver Crown, struck in Ireland in 1643 during the viceroyalty of James, Marquis (later Duke) of Ormonde.
59. Silver Crown of the Commonwealth (1649–60), the only period in history when a range of coins was struck for circulation in England with the full legend in English.

copper from about 1574, but these coins did not appear for general circulation. Finally, a proclamation was drafted, though it was probably not published, prohibiting the tokens but legalising a limited tender of halfpenny and farthing pledges, which were made of pure copper.

Two further events of importance, which were to have a profound significance in the time ahead, were to take place in the reign of Elizabeth I. The first of these was an attempt to introduce the new method of coining by the mill and screw press which, as already mentioned, had been used in France, coming there from Italy. Milled coins of gold and silver were struck, and went into circulation alongside the hammered coins; but again, the time was not yet. Many such pieces still exist and are available to collectors.

Finally, trade with India was by now an economic asset worth developing. It promised to become of even greater importance, as did overseas trade as a whole; England had long contested the right to sail to and trade with the Americas and to settle there. For use in the East a new coin was issued, the second event of importance, since it may be regarded as the first English attempt as a 'colonial' coinage. It did not carry the portrait of Elizabeth, only the portcullis, the badge of the Beauforts, which was adopted by the House of Tudor.

The largest piece was the crown-sized Eight Testernes, and, with its subdivisions, it is now quite rare. It did not find favour and the issue was stopped; but viewing the general picture of the coinage and colonial development, the series marks a new stage in which the country was soon to be called upon to provide money for its territories overseas. This piece and others in the colonial series are referred to in Chapter Nine.

The coinage of James I (1603–25) holds much that is of interest to the numismatist. As will be seen (from Appendix I and II) there was an unusually large variety of coins issued, and a number of collections devoted to this reign have been formed at various times.

Many historians have had considerable sympathy for James. His early life was one of considerable personal danger. Few children have had a more unsettled childhood or early life, and the conditions under which he was reared, the instability of his father and to some extent of his mother, left marks upon his mentality that he was to carry throughout his life. He suffered measures of frustration, not the least in his writings, which he considered of great scholarly importance, but which never attained that measure of serious consideration which he felt to be their due.

One of the outstanding historical events of the reign was the union of the thrones of England and Scotland. The political union was not to take place till the time of Queen Anne; James actually reigned over two separate kingdoms, but this was the first occasion on which a king was to occupy both the thrones of England and Scotland at the same time.

This fact was reflected in the legends on the coinage, one of the favourites being EXURGAT DEUS DISSIPENTUR INIMICI ('Let God arise and let His enemies be scattered') on the larger gold coins of the first issue, and TUEATUR UNITA DEUS ('God protect the union') on the smaller. Similar legends, as HENRICUS ROSAS REGNA IACOBUS ('Henry united the roses, James the realms') and FACIAM EOS IN GENTEM UNAM ('I will make of them one nation'), had the same purpose in mind. These two legends occur on coins of the second issue together with QUAE DEUS CONIUNXIT NEMO SEPARET ('What God hath joined let no man put asunder') on the silver coins.

The coinage periods are three in number, from 1603 to 1604, from 1604 to 1619 and from 1619 to 1625. The issue of gold was considerable, thirteen denominations being struck, and a large number of mint marks used.

Die varieties for the various denominations are considerable. Some may have arisen from the fact that James took a personal interest in his coinage, selected some of the religious legends himself, and visited the Mint, where he made other suggestions relative to the designs.

In the last issue of gold coins the head of James is shown wearing a laurel wreath. This is the first time the Roman style of laurel wreath appeared on the head of a king on the coinage, and the piece, a unit (halves and quarters were also issued), soon got to be known as a 'Laurel'. The idea arose from James's delight in being represented as the 'Cæsar Augustus' of Britain, which title he assumed on his coronation medal.

In passing, it might be noted that the reign of James I was the first in which an official coronation commemorative medal was issued by the Mint for distribution to the public. This practice was continued till the present reign when it was suddenly dropped, the gap being filled by a privately struck medal. Such coronation medals were usually in gold and silver, bronze medals also being added at a later date. Those who felt that the coronation commemorative crown of 1953 was too medallic in appearance no doubt regretted the lack of an official medal and felt that the crown failed by trying to be both coin and medal.

The coins of the first issue of James I were the sovereign and half, and the crown and half-crown and the quarter-angel. Angels and half-angels were coined but are not known. In the silver series, crowns and half-crowns, shillings and sixpences, half-groats, pennies and halfpennies were struck, and on the coins of this issue James is styled as King of England, France and Ireland. In the second issue of coins the title of the king was changed to 'King of Great Britain' (etc.), an innovation which was to be carried on through many future reigns.

A difficulty which always has to be contended with in coin-

Plate 13 ENGLISH COINS: CHARLES II, QUEEN ANNE

60. Simon's famous silver 'Petition Crown'. His petition to the king was inscribed in two lines on the edge of the coin.
61. Gold Five-Guinea piece of Charles II (1660–85). The elephant below the bust indicates that the gold came from Guinea in Africa, from which the guinea range of coins takes its popular name.
62. Gold Guinea of Queen Anne (1702–14). The word VIGO below the bust indicates that the coin was struck from gold captured at the battle of Vigo Bay.

CAROLVS II DEI GRA
16 63 MAG BRI FR ET HIB REX
CAROLVS·II· DEI·GRATIA
16 68 MAG BR·FRA·ET·HIB·REX
ANNA DEI GRATIA
17 05 MAG BR FRA ET HIB REG
60
61
62

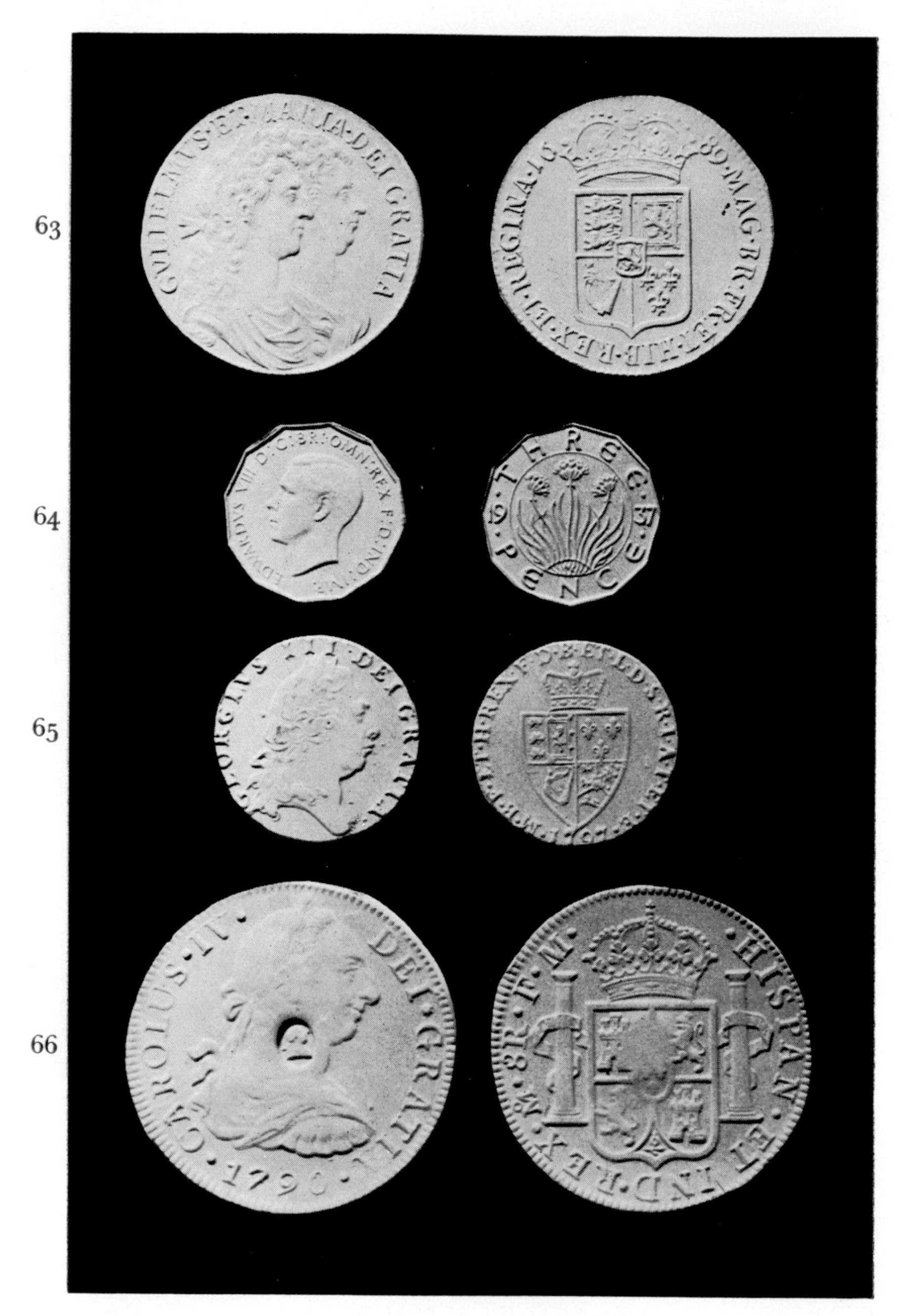
63
GVLIELMVS·ET·MARIA·DEI·GRATIA
16 89·MAG·BR·FR·ET·HIB·REX·ET·REGINA
64
THREE PENCE
19 37
65
66
CAROLUS·IV·DEI·GRATIA·1790
HISPAN·ET IND·REX
8R·F·M

age matters is the export of coinage from its country of origin to some other where its metal value is greater than in its own land. Naturally, gold is particularly susceptible to export, and though regulations have been enacted, penalties imposed and coins revalued, the practice of exporting coins has continued down to our own times.

In the times of James I the difficulties in this respect were no less acute, and in 1604 new gold coins of reduced weight were issued in an attempt to put an end to the practice. The attempt failed, and a commission was appointed in 1609 to suggest a further remedy. In 1611 the value of all gold was raised by 10 per cent, and gold coins if short in weight by two grains in ten shillings were demonetised. This also proved ineffective and a new coinage was issued in 1619, the third issue referred to above. Another purpose of the new coinage was to remove the difficulties which had arisen due to the necessity for fractional reckonings owing to the rise of 10 per cent in the value of the gold coins.

In silver, the crown with the equestrian figure of the King continued to be issued, with the half-crown, shilling, sixpence, half-groat (2*d.*), penny and halfpenny.

Plate 14 ENGLISH COINS: WILLIAM AND MARY, EDWARD VIII, GEORGE III

63. Silver Half-crown of William and Mary (1689–94). Joint monarchs, their busts were shown side by side, a unique feature of the coins of this reign.
64. Nickel-brass Threepence of Edward VIII (1936). Prepared for circulation in 1937 the design is very similar to that eventually adopted on the same coin of George VI.
65. The well-known 'Spade' Guinea of George III (1760–1820). So called from the shape of the shield on the reverse, this coin, still bearing the French arms as part of its heraldic device, is the commonest guinea in the English guinea series.
66. Silver Eight-Reales piece of Charles IV of Spain, countermarked with the head of George III. The piece circulated in England during a great shortage of silver coin.

The matter of copper coinage was still unsettled and some attempt at a solution of the problem was now made. The efforts which had been made in the reign of Elizabeth I to stop the issue of copper tokens had proved unsuccessful. James decided to accept the necessity and an issue of copper farthings commenced. These were not struck by the Mint. A patent was given to Lord Harington by which he was authorised to issue copper farthings in the king's name. The coins have on them two sceptres, crowned, on one side and a crowned harp on the other, as well as bearing mint or privy marks. They vary somewhat in size, and some which are oval in shape are thought by some authorities to have been intended for circulation in Ireland. Now that the issue was authorised it met with considerable resistance, though it had been enacted that the acceptance of the pieces might not be forced.

Lord Harington died in the year in which the patent was granted and it was sold by his widow in 1615 to the Duke of Lennox. On his death it passed to his widow, the Duchess of Richmond. We thus have an issue of small copper coins, legal for the first time, known under the names of Harington, Lennox and Richmond farthings, according to the date of issue. The issue extended into the next reign, and in 1624 the patent passed to Lord Maltravers, whose name is thus added to the list. In 1623 a rose replaced the harp on the reverse. Strange as it may seem, these pieces were forged to a fairly serious extent, and to check this a brass centre was latterly set into the copper.

There are many collectors who specialise in copper coins alone. English coppers are of considerable interest as a series and in the main are not expensive to collect. There is ample scope for study: there are many types and varieties over the sequence of reigns and many interesting background stories occur from time to time. Probably that best known is of the Duchess of Richmond who, in the reign of Charles II, sat as the model for the figure of Britannia. Adapted from the Britannia of the Roman type of the second century, this symbolic figure has appeared on the reverse of many of the copper and bronze coins consistently from 1672.

The official regular issues in copper, therefore, started with

James I. From the farthings then issued were to develop the bronze coins of today. Their striking has often been carried out by private firms under contract to the Mint. For the British Museum catalogue, compiled by Mr. Wilson Peck, see Chapter Eight.

It was enacted that the first issues of farthings were to be sold by the patentee at a 10 per cent surplus in twenty shillings and to be similarly redeemed. They were struck from strips of metal, and at least one strip has survived in which the coins are still all joined together with the waste metal surrounding them.

In 1616 a permanent exchange was established for them in London, at which they were discounted for silver coins. Taking the picture as a whole, the early copper coins got away to a rather bad start, and it may be, as mentioned before, that the wheel has now almost turned full circle. With farthings now demonetised, and no pennies issued for some years, the time for a new base metal coinage may well be upon us. What it may be gives rise to speculation. Tin has been used for some of the minor denominations, half-pennies and farthings, in the reigns of Charles II, James II and William and Mary. In our own times aluminium has been tried for certain colonial minor coins, such as the one-tenth of a penny of British West Africa. Steel and iron were tried in the German financial collapse of the 1920's, a metal named Tombak was issued in Canada and the States during the Second World War, but none seems to have proved as satisfactory for the purpose as copper or bronze. As stated, man-made plastics are hinted at, but even these would not be quite a new departure. The London County Council, Glasgow, Leeds, Southampton, Sheffield, Aberdeen, Birmingham, Bury, and Dundee all issued such plastic fare tokens for their tramways in the period 1880–1900.

It has already been said that the number of denominations issued during the reign of James I was considerable. To detail them all here would be wearisome; the reader will find them set forth with reasonable clarity in the Appendix.

In the latter part of the reign the production of silver from mines in Wales was considerable, and certain coins of the third issue carry a Welsh plume over the shield as an indication of the source of the metal.

References to this practice and to similar cases will be made again from time to time. It is not perhaps realised that many early English coins were struck in gold and silver which was produced in commercial quantities at this period within the British Isles. The amount produced was not necessarily sufficient to meet the complete demand for coinage purposes, but it supplied a considerable proportion of the metal required.

We have now reached the stage where much of British coin metal comes from abroad by purchase. Nickel is not mined in Great Britain, and the gold and silver which still remains is so small in amount as to be hardly a commercial proposition. Much of interest might be written on various sources of supply of coin metal which have been used during English history. Briefly, they might be summarised as (*a*) metal mined in the British Isles; (*b*) metal originally used for other purposes, such as gold and silver ornaments and table silver; (*c*) bullion captured from enemy sources; (*d*) metal imported from Dominions and Colonies or from occupied countries; (*e*) metal purchased from private companies engaged in mining, both at home and in the Dominions and Colonies; (*f*) metal purchased from miscellaneous sources or obtained by exchange or barter; (*g*) metal brought into the country, usually in the form of foreign coin, as a dowry or indemnity or in payment of debts. As our story proceeds many of these sources will be mentioned in due place and period.

4. CHARLES I

There are very many to whom the subject of history is one which they approach with a certain amount of respect. There are still more who, having little or no knowledge of early history, take up a book such as this with a certain amount of misgiving, since it commences with some aspects of the earliest history of England. From the numismatist's point of view these misgivings of the unknown or unappreciated do not exist. He can take up his subject at any point in time that he may choose and, if he so desires, carry on from there or confine his studies to the one particular period in which he has an interest or of which he has some particular knowledge or appreciation.

We have now arrived in our brief studies at the reign of Charles I (1625–49), and there are many for whom the history of Britain commences at this point. The period is within grasp of our understanding: it is not so far removed as to appear to have little or no relation to things which we know and can appreciate.

In writing of the history of English coinage it is hard to refrain from repeating that some period is of particular interest, but that of Charles I has its own special appeal. The reader, if he be so minded, may well commence this book at the point at which it has now arrived without the feeling that he has been in any way remiss in not probing that which has gone before.

For we are now on the brink of those eras of English history which have the most popular appeal to those who make no pretensions to wide historical knowledge, those who prefer a period which, popularised by many historical works of both fact and fiction, offers something which is within grasp of modern times.

And what a colourful period in history this is! Houses and cottages are still standing and inhabited – as a part of everyday life – in which some small part of the history of this period was enacted. Typical of such is Moseley Old Hall near Wolverhampton, scene in 1960 of some modest Restoration celebrations. Hidden down a quiet byway, it is worthy of a visit. In such places hoards of coins, concealed during the troubles of this time, are still to be found.

For in this period a state existed which is naturally foreign to our nature, a state of civil war: a state which the English can appreciate but which they hardly expect to recur. Civil wars have now turned themselves into periods of industrial strife: probably the General Strike of the 1920's is as near as we are likely to come again to civil strife.

As always in unsettled times, the state of the country is reflected in the coinage, and the reign of Charles I is no exception, being remarkable for a number of unprecedented issues. In this instance one of the forms which such issues took was the extensive striking of siege pieces, issued by towns surrounded by the Parliamentary forces.

The coins current during the reign were, for this and other

reasons, of some complexity. Here again there have been many collectors who specialised in the coins of this reign alone. Charles came to the throne in March 1625, and for a short time the work of the Mint was continued with the dies of James I. At the pyx trial which took place in July the coins submitted bore the portrait and titles of James.

The Mint was at once beset with troubles. Work had hardly begun on the new coinage when an epidemic of the Plague seriously interfered with production. At the same time the gold coins which had been brought over as a part of the dowry of Henrietta Maria, sister of Louis XIII of France and Queen Consort of Charles I, were about to be recoined in the English style. The difficulties experienced with this recoining and the onset of the Plague caused some of the coins, the *quart d'ecu*, to be put into circulation as they were received. This only continued for a short time.

By the time the Civil War broke out in 1642, the coinage was fully established. Gold, silver and copper were issued, the latter under conditions already referred to. Some issues of the coinage were considerably influenced by Nicholas Briot, a Frenchman who had been attached to the Paris Mint, and who came to this country in 1625 and obtained employment at the Royal Mint in the Tower. He was commissioned in 1628 to design portraits for both coins and medals. He reintroduced into England the latest French machinery, with the mill and screw press that had formerly been used in the reign of Elizabeth I. With this machinery he was able to produce a round coin of very fine workmanship. Viewing the coins of the reign as a whole, the contrast is very great between the fine coins of Briot, and some of the other issues from the provincial Mints during the war, which are as rough in workmanship and striking as any in our history.

Briot appears to have worked at the Tower for two periods of twelve months, 1631–32 and 1638–39. In the interval he filled an appointment at the Scottish Mint, from 1635 till 1637. His coins are easily distinguished, not only by their fine workmanship and regular shape but by Briot's privy mark, a flower and a 'B' or an anchor and a 'B'. Though James I had united the two thrones, both England and Scotland still had their own separate coinage, of somewhat similar appearance but of different denominational values.

Just as Eloye Mestrell, who introduced milled coins in the reign of Elizabeth I, was to encounter hostility from the employees at the Mint, so Briot encountered similar opposition. He was, as it turned out, to have an adventurous career. When it became evident that civil war was inevitable, one of the actions of Charles was to summon Briot to York and to direct that a cargo of mint machinery should be shipped thither so that the national coinage could be carried on. This valuable cargo never reached its destination, being captured at Scarborough by the Parliamentary forces. Briot, by whatever means, managed to get the York Mint into operation, and while, during the Civil War, he was still employed at the Tower, he continued to work for the King also, both there and later at Oxford. It is probable that the York Mint remained in operation till 1644, when the city fell to the Parliamentary forces after the Battle of Marston Moor.

While the Civil War was being fought, mints appeared at a considerable number of provincial towns or in provincial castles, and thus reflect the changing fortunes of the Royalist party. At various times mints were in operation at the following places: York, 1642–44; Aberystwyth, 1638–42; and again from January to March 1646; Combe Martin, 1647–48; Shrewsbury, October to December 1642; Oxford, 1643–46; Bristol, 1643–45; Truro, 1642–43; Exeter, 1643–46; Weymouth, 1643–44; Sandsfoot Castle, probably in operation for only a short time before being moved to Weymouth; Worcester (Hartlebury Castle), 1646; Chester, 1644.

As will be seen, in some cases these provincial mints were in operation for a few months, and it will also be noted that Aberystwyth mint was in operation for its first period before the Civil War commenced on August 22, 1642. Nor did all the provincial mints strike every denomination; many of them did not strike gold coins at all.

Welsh silver was again used for some of the coinage, and was normally transported to London for the purpose. In 1637 Thomas Bushell, the then lessee of the Welsh silver mines, was authorised to establish the Aberystwyth mint, which, as noted above, came into operation in the next year. Bushell used an open book as his mint mark.

As in other cases, with his removal of the mint to another town, the open book mint mark was issued from mints other than Aberystwyth, the mint mark in this case being that of the striker of coins, not that of the place in which they were struck. The first period of minting at Aberystwyth continued till the day after the King's Declaration at Wellington in Shropshire, when Bushell moved his mint to Shrewsbury. His open book mint mark went with him, and later Bushell again moved his mint to Oxford where, as stated, Briot had a hand in the design and production of the coins.

This process of moving mints about resulted in some apparent anomalies in the use of mint marks and in the production of a considerable number of 'mules'. Coins are so named when they are struck from a die specially made for, or associated with, one particular mint or period, used in conjunction with another die associated with a different mint or period.

Though Shrewsbury mint was only in operation for a short period before being transferred to the king's headquarters at

Plate 15 ENGLISH COINS: GEORGE III

67. Silver Eight-Reales piece of Spain, planed smooth and re-struck as a Bank of England Dollar of 1804, during the shortage of silver coin.
68. Gold Sovereign of George III (1760–1820). Re-equipped with new machinery by Boulton and Watt, the Royal Mint set about remedying the shortage of coin. The coinage was revalued, placing the Guinea at a premium, and Sovereigns took their place.
69. Silver Crown of George III. Pistrucci's famous 'St. George and the Dragon' appears within the Garter on the reverse.

GEORGIUS III DEI GRATIA REX
BANK OF ENGLAND
FIVE SHILLINGS
DOLLAR
1804
67
68
GEORGIUS III D: G: BRITANNIARUM REX F: D:
1818
HONI SOIT QUI MAL Y PENSE
69

Plate 16

70
GEORGIUS III·D·G·REX.
BRITANNIA.
1797
71
FOUR PENCE
1836
72
VICTORIA DEI GRATIA
1839
DIRIGE DEUS GRESSUS MEOS.
MDCCCXXXIX.

Oxford (December 1642), coins of two interesting types were struck at this mint for the first time. Of these, the first was a series of coins with the reverse redesigned to incorporate part of the king's famous Declaration. The words RELIGIO PROTESTANTIUM, LEGES ANGLIÆ, LIBERTAS PARLIAMENTI (the religion of the Protestants, the laws of England, the liberty of the Parliament) were incorporated in various abbreviated forms, usually in two lines across the field of the reverse. In view of his activities before the outbreak of war, his ruling for eleven years without Parliament, his attempted arrest of the Five Members when Parliament did meet, and some of his attempted religious 'reforms', it can hardly be wondered at that this pious Declaration was not accepted on all sides as of any value. Its use on coins does demonstrate how money, the main commodity likely to pass through everyone's hands, could be used as a form of propaganda spreader.

Secondly, from the Shrewsbury mint began the issue of large silver pieces current at one pound and half a pound, which were struck in this metal to make good the shortage of gold coins. Gold, however, still continued to be minted during the Civil War period. In some cases, as at the Battle of Edgehill, the unit

Plate 16 ENGLISH COINS: GEORGE III, WILLIAM IV, VICTORIA

70. Struck by private contractors, Messrs. Boulton and Watt at their Soho Mint, Birmingham, these Twopenny pieces weighed two ounces and had incuse legends on a broad 'cartwheel' rim.
71. An attempt to revive the Groat for general circulation resulted in the striking of the 'Britannia' Fourpence in the reign of William IV (1830–37). The coin lasted into the next reign (Victoria) but was then discontinued, apart from the Maundy Groat, which is still struck.
72. A handsome pattern Five-Pound piece in gold, this design of the reign of Victoria (1837–1901) was not adopted for coins for general circulation. The reverse shows the Queen as Una, leading the British lion

or gold pound-piece was given to officers as a form of medal for services rendered.

A symbol incorporated over many reigns, for showing the origin of the coin metal to be Wales, is the plume of three feathers. Generally, where this symbol appears on a silver coin the deduction as to its origin is a safe one. Owing to the Civil War, the metal of which the coins of Charles I are struck came from many sources other than the mines of the Principality.

In June 1642, as a result of a demand for gold and silver plate for coinage purposes, vast quantities were deposited at Guildhall, London. This was a foreshadow of events to come. Between July and November, after the declaration of war in August, the king received at Nottingham, Shrewsbury and Oxford large quantities of plate, in the latter case from the Colleges, and from general private sources.

Oxford remained a mint from 1642 till the town surrendered and the king fled to Newark in 1646. Its situation was such that a considerable amount of Welsh silver succeeded in reaching the Oxford mint, as it did the mints of Aberystwyth and Shrewsbury. At Oxford, Thomas Bushell produced in 1644 what has become the celebrated and rare Oxford Crown. This shows the king on horseback, still the general obverse type for the larger coins, with a view of the city of Oxford seen below the horse.

From Oxford Bushell proceeded under orders to Bristol, where on the capture of that city by the Royalists in 1643 he set up a mint. Here coins from the half-crown to the penny were struck in silver, as well as the unite and half-unite in gold. These coins can usually be distinguished by the presence of the letters BR in the form of a monogram.

It seems probable that certain coins of the Bristol type were struck elsewhere after the town fell to the Parliamentary forces in September 1645. Such coins, though associated by reason of their appearance with Bristol, are marked with an 'A' or 'B' letter. From this it has been suggested that Bushell transferred the mint to Appledore and then to Barnstaple, but from the fact that Bushell was Governor of Lundy Island it is sometimes considered that the mint was eventually set up there.

With the plate which had been collected and with the Welsh mines in the rear of his headquarters, it was possible for Charles to authorise more than one mint to operate when conditions were favourable, and thus to supply the west of England with money at a time when transport of bullion or coin was fraught with some danger. In 1642 he commissioned Sir Richard Vyvyan to strike gold and silver coins at such places as he might see fit. Truro was the place chosen, and a trunk-load of plate was conveyed thither from Liskeard to supply the necessary bullion. In 1643 Exeter fell to the Royalist party and the mint was transferred there, where it operated till the city again fell to the Parliamentary forces in 1646. Coins of both mints are recognisable by their distinctive types and mint marks.

Such documents as may have existed authorising the mint at Weymouth have failed to survive. The mint was only in operation from September 1643 till June 1644, having, as stated, probably been transferred there from Sandsfoot Castle. Its coins are quite distinctive, some having a 'W' on them by way of mint mark. Some also have the letters 'SA', but most of these are attributed either to Sandsfoot Castle or to the continuance of the use of the dies of that mint at Weymouth. Some Weymouth coins have traces of the 'SA' on the dies, though this has been erased and the coins themselves are generally of very rough workmanship.

Of even shorter duration was the mint at Worcester, where coins were struck at Hartlebury Castle and have the letters 'HC'. Only the half-crown was struck, with the mint mark of a pear or three pears, taken from the county arms. The coins belong to the period of the siege of Worcester, March to July 1646. Though the attribution of HC to Hartlebury has gained acceptance it is still unproved. Documentary evidence is lacking. Though Hartlebury is some 12 miles from Worcester the circumstantial evidence appears favourable.

Another mint of shorter duration, though it was to appear again in a later reign, was Chester. This mint too struck half-crowns, distinguished by the mint mark of three wheatsheaves, sometimes known as gerbs, and the letters CHST below the horse. The mint owes its origin to an order dated January 31, 1644, which directed that £100 of plate was to be converted into coin for the defence of the city and the payment of debts. These coins, along with many other of the Civil War issues, are rare.

So far nothing has been said of the Tower Mint during the war period. It continued to issue coin throughout but, though it may seem strange, made no material alterations to the types, which still continued to show the king in effigy. This was due to the necessity that existed for the universal acceptance of the money itself. The practice of striking apparently regal coins continued until the king's death. The mint marks used, 'P', '(P)' and '(R)', usually denote the Parliamentary Tower issues, though an eye was used in 1645, the sun from 1645 till 1646, and the sceptre from then till 1649.

Finally, a word must be said about the siege pieces, the obsidional issues of the towns and castles sometime in a state of siege during the war. Such pieces were issued at Carlisle, Colchester, Newark, Pontefract and Scarborough. At one time it was thought that Beeston Castle also issued siege pieces, but later research points to the fact that the soldiers there had plenty of money, making such issues apparently unnecessary.

The coins themselves are often of unusual denominations and irregular shape. Most of them were cut direct from pieces of plate, of which a few bear traces such as hall marks or mould-

Plate 17 ENGLISH COINS: VICTORIA

73. Agitation for the decimalisation of the English coinage resulted in the striking of a silver tenth-of-a-pound piece in 1849. Known as the Florin, it was quickly named 'Godless' since the letters D.G. (*Dei Gratia*, by the Grace of God) were omitted from the legend. The design reflects the Gothic revival of the period.
74. The 'Gothic' Florin of Victoria, with D.G. restored and the date in Roman numerals (Silver).
75. Gold 'Jubilee' Five-Pound piece of Victoria, issued in 1887. This portrait of the queen was not popular and resulted in the next design.
76. Gold Two-Pound piece of Victoria. The obverse design gave the coin the name of the 'old head' type.

VICTORIA D:G: BRITT:REG:F:D:
1887
VICTORIA·DEI·GRA·BRITT·REGINA·FID·DEF·IND·IMP
1893
73
74
75
76

Plate 18

77
VICTORIA D:G: BRITT:REG:F:D:
ONE PENNY
1860
78
EDWARDVS VII D:G: BRITT:OMN: REX F:D: IND: IMP:
ONE FLORIN TWO SHILLINGS
1902
79
GEORGIVS V D.G.BRITT:OMN:REX F.D.IND:IMP:
1913
80
GEORGIVS VI D:G:BR:OMN:REX
FID DEF
1951
ONE SHILLING

ings. Carlisle, for example, which was besieged from October 1644 till June 1645, struck three-shilling pieces and shillings in silver, either octagonal or almost round in shape. Colchester, besieged from June till August 1648, struck an almost round ten-shilling piece in gold, showing the gateway of the castle; while Newark, which was besieged several times, issued half-crowns, shillings and ninepences in 1645 and 1646 and sixpences in 1646. These pieces are lozenge-shaped.

Pontefract, besieged from June 1648 till March 1649, struck lozenge-shaped two shillings and lozenge-shaped, octagonal and round shillings, showing the castle, with a hand brandishing a defiant sword protruding from one of the windows. After the death of Charles I a second issue was made, with the legend CAROLVS SECVUNDVS, and this piece showed a cannon in place of the hand and sword. Of both issues a few specimens are known in gold.

Scarborough, besieged from July 1644 till July 1645, issued coins of various shapes, some of them showing the castle. In some cases this is shown incuse, that is, stamped into the coin, and in others the castle appears in relief. Scarborough is mainly

Plate 18 ENGLISH COINS: VICTORIA, EDWARD VII, GEORGE V, GEORGE VI

77. Bronze Penny of Victoria (1837–1901). This coin quickly became known as the 'bun' penny, from the queen's hair style. It also established a legend that a ship and a lighthouse ought to appear on the English penny. The ship dates back to the 1797 copper series.
78. Silver Florin of Edward VII (1901–10). The lady representing Britannia is Lady Susan Hicks-Beach, daughter of the then Deputy Master of the Royal Mint. She appeared on millions of coins, and was thus portrayed more times than any modern film star.
79. Gold Sovereign of George V (1910–36). The last reign in which gold coins were struck for circulation in England.
80. Cupro-nickel Shilling of George VI (1936–52). Known as the 'Scottish' shilling by reason of the reverse design, it was introduced as a silver piece in 1937 as a compliment to the then Queen Consort, now Queen Elizabeth the Queen Mother. It was struck in London, and has continued to appear ever since.

notable for its great variety of denominations, unrivalled in Great Britain except perhaps in the case of James VI of Scotland. These denominations seem calculated to meet almost any need without the necessity of giving change, a circumstance which would be readily appreciated during a great shortage of actual specie. They consist of 5*s*., 3*s*. 4*d*., 2*s*. 10*d*., 2*s*. 6*d*., 2*s*. 4*d*., 2*s*., 1*s*. 9*d*., 1*s*. 6*d*., 1*s*. 4*d*., 1*s*. 3*d*., 1*s*. 2*d*., 1*s*. 1*d*., 1*s*., 11*d*., 10*d*., 7*d*., 6*d*, and 4*d*. The reason for this extensive range is that the blanks were cut from articles of plate, then weighed and finally stamped with a value appropriate to this weight.

At the same time the Civil War extended to Ireland, then still under direct rule from England but, like Scotland, having its own separate coinage, as it did from A.D. 979 till 1830, when its coinage was assimilated to that of Great Britain till 1928. In Ireland the Civil War was known as the 'Irish Rebellion'. Similar emergency coins, known as 'money of necessity', were struck there. They were mainly pieces of plate, suitably marked. They are rather more rough in appearance than many of the English siege pieces of the period, and were ultimately issued by both sides. Their primary object was for the relief of the Government and the payment of the army sent to suppress the rebels. The issues were from Inchiquin, 1642, Dublin, 1642, Kilkenny, 1642, 'Blacksmith's' money, so called on account of its very rough workmanship, 1642, Ormonde money, Rebel money, 1643, and Cork money, 1647. As will be seen, some of the series were issued by localities and others by various lords, such as Inchiquin, and the Viceroy, James, Marquis (later Duke) of Ormonde.

5. COMMONWEALTH TO WILLIAM IV

There is probably no more dreary period in English history than that of the Commonwealth. Colour and pageantry were drained out of life, many works of art were destroyed, and much that was irreplaceable vanished for ever.

As always, the state of national affairs was reflected in the coinage. The coins of the Commonwealth are not remarkable either for their execution or artistic appeal. One good thing did occur, a considerable simplification of the coinage with regard to the series of denominations issued. Reference to the Appendix will show the multitudinous types and forms of denomination so far issued during some of the reigns which have passed.

It has been a matter of some surprise to historians that such an ugly coinage should have been adopted, since the post of graver to the Mint was in the hands of Thomas Simon, about whom we shall hear more later. Undoubtedly one of the greatest of English medallists, it seems probable that the work of the coinage must have been left in the hands of his assistants, East and Burgh.

In this period we see the emergence of a small but adequate number of denominations, the unite or broad of twenty shillings, the half-unite or ten shillings, known also as the half-broad or double-crown, and the crown, all gold coins. In silver the crown, half-crown, shilling, sixpence, half-groat, penny and halfpenny met the demand for smaller denominations.

After the death of the king the coinage order of 1649 laid down, amongst other things, that the legends on the coins were to be in English, thus abandoning the Latin which had become traditional many reigns before. Indeed, the coinage was as utilitarian as it could be. To obviate any chance of mistake, not only was the English legend adopted but the value of the coin was placed on each. Though this had been done before with some denominations it was now adopted as universal. Little possibility of error remained.

Simon, after some years of full engagement on the seals and medals of the period, was at last able to turn his attention to the coinage. Though the unpleasing designs had of necessity been suffered by the public, unfavourable comment had not been wanting, and Simon's coins showed some return to higher artistic standards. With the help of the mill machinery installed by Blondeau he produced a fine set of coins. In this issue the broad in gold was valued at fifty shillings, and a series of smaller denominations down to the sixpence in silver completed the range. These coins had the bust of the Protector on the obverse, and Latin reappeared in the wording of the legend. Though they had been struck by the order of Cromwell, the pieces were not officially put into circulation, though there are some pieces which appear to have been so used. A farthing in copper, the only piece of this metal for the period, was also struck.

The deficiency and, during the Commonwealth period, the total absence of copper coins continued to be a burden. As a result, traders took it into their own hands to issue a copper token coinage, generally known as seventeenth-century tradesman's tokens. These pieces were in use between 1648 and 1672, and form a matter of individual numismatic interest in themselves. During the latter part of the period their issue assumed vast proportions, and they appeal to many collectors since they became almost official and circulated freely. Much local town and parish history is bound up with them and they are, in the main, inexpensive to collect. More details of such issues will be found in Chapter Eight.

There is little more that needs to be said about this uninspiring period. Great changes were upon the country and no less upon the coinage with the coming Restoration of the Monarchy.

After the drabness of the Commonwealth the balance swung, perhaps, too far the other way. We have seen such things happen after major wars; in such circumstances a considerable reaction can be expected.

Thus with the Restoration. The coinage too was about to undergo what is perhaps the greatest change in its history. As has been recorded, milled coins had been experimented with from time to time since the reign of Elizabeth I. After due consideration it was now decided that in future this type of coin alone should be the standard issue for England. Both the great contemporary diarists Evelyn and Pepys make some mention of this great change, in which both had some personal interest.

It naturally took some time for such a major change to come to fruition. It will be no surprise that the first issues of the new reign were produced by the hammer method. In denominational values these issues followed for the last time the now familiar pattern of a broad or twenty shillings, with half-broad and crown in gold. The silver issues continued with much the same titles as before, half-crown, shilling, sixpence, groat, threepence, half-groat and penny being struck. The absence of a silver crown will be noticed.

It may be well to sketch very briefly again the origins of milled coins in this country. They first arrived in the reign of Elizabeth I, when Mestrell, who had been employed at the French mint, was engaged at the Royal Mint in the Tower in 1561. His new methods met with opposition, and the system of striking ceased in 1572. Nicholas Briot (1579–1646) was appointed Chief Engraver at the Royal Mint in 1633, and he improved the mechanical method of striking coins. Examples of his work have been reviewed in the reign of Charles I. Peter Blondeau, also from France, was invited over by the Government in 1649. Again the foreigner met with opposition, which finally resulted in Warrants being issued to Blondeau and Ramage to prepare patterns of milled coins, which were to be submitted for the consideration of the council. Though Blondeau's work seems mainly, so far as improvements were concerned, to have been related to the marking of the edges of the coins, his patterns were of finer work than those of Ramage. Opposition became so strong eventually that Blondeau had to resign, returning to France with a pension of £100. Cromwell's milled coins were probably struck on the machinery which Blondeau had used at the Tower.

At the Restoration Charles II invited Blondeau to return, confirmed his pension and appointed him Provost of the moneyers and engravers at the Mint, a post he was to hold for some fourteen years. As already stated, all this improvement was concentrated mainly on the attempt to strike coins which would defy the artifices of the clipper and forger. Since Blondeau's improvements concerned mainly the edges of the coins which, by his process, could either be lettered or grained, and since the coins themselves were almost truly circular and of even thickness, the problem as it then existed was practically solved.

Thus by gradual development and experiment a stage had been reached when it was practical for the change to machine-made coins to be introduced. An agreement was signed; Blondeau was responsible for the production of coins of even weight and thickness, of regular shape and constant size for each denomination. As a further protection against clipping, he was to introduce his process whereby the coins were struck in a collar which, as well as keeping them regular in shape, would mark their edges with either a legend or with suitable graining. It will no doubt have been realised that the word 'engines' had a wider meaning at this time than it has since acquired, and was applied to almost any form of machine.

The agreement signed, the next matter was the actual design of the coins themselves. Thomas Simon was still the chief engraver at the Mint, and he and John Roettier of Antwerp entered into competition for the work of making the dies for the new coinage. Patterns were prepared, Roettier's were preferred, and he was entrusted with the work. Simon put up a fight for his position. When the new coins appeared in 1662 he issued a few specimens of his pattern crown with a petition legend on the edge. This 'Petition Crown', dated 1663, bore considerable resemblance to the work of Roettier, and on the edge were the words: THOMAS SIMON MOST HUMBLY PRAYS YOUR MAJESTY TO COMPARE THIS HIS TRYALL PIECE WITH THE DUTCH AND IF MORE TRVLY DRAWN & EMBOSS'D MORE GRACE FVLLY ORDER'D AND MORE ACCURATELY ENGRAVEN TO RELIEVE HIM. When it is realised that these words, with the name of the artist and the word 'Majesty' in script, with each word spaced out with a stop, were placed on the edge of a crown-piece in a double ring of lettering, it will be seen that the production of the piece was no mean achievement. He also issued two other pattern crowns, known as 'Reddite' crowns, similar in appearance but with the legend RENDER UNTO CÆSAR THE THINGS WHICH ARE CÆSAR'S, etc., in either English or Latin. The official decision remained unshaken: Roettier was not displaced.

From 1662 until 1816–17 the denominations now put into use remained constant. They were five guineas, two guineas, guinea and half-guinea in gold, with the occasional appearance of quarter and third guineas; crown, half-crown, shilling, sixpence, fourpence, threepence, twopence and penny in silver. From this period, 1662, the latter four coins are usually associated with Maundy money, of which more later. Halfpennies and farthings in copper and a few in tin also appeared, but the now familiar copper penny was not to arrive before 1797.

As will be seen the guinea was the unit, with multiples and subdivisions, and the custom was carried on of marking the coins to show the origin of the metal. The name 'guinea' comes in fact from Guinea in Africa, from which place the gold for the coins was now arriving.

The main markings to show origin during the period 1662 to 1816 were as follows:

An elephant or an elephant and castle: metal from the Africa Company.
Plumes: metal from the Welsh mines.
A rose: metal from the west of England mines.
The word VIGO: coins struck from bullion captured at the Battle of Vigo Bay, 1702.
The word LIMA: coins struck from metal captured by Lord Anson and by various privateers in or about the year 1743, mainly from Spanish treasure ships. See *Numismatic Circular* (Spink and Son), London, 1963.
The letters E.I.C.: coins struck either for the East India Company or from metal sent by that Company to the Mint.
Roses and plumes: coins struck from metal supplied by the 'Company for smelting down lead'.
The letters W.C.C.: coins struck from metal supplied by the Welsh Copper Company.
The letters S.S.C.: coins struck from metal supplied by the famous South Sea Company.

One or two other marks occur in this period of milled coinage history. Hammered coins in increasingly bad condition continued to circulate till 1696. They were then called in and replaced by a large issue of milled money. This necessitated considerable work for the Mint, and to ease pressure on the Tower, branch mints were opened at Bristol, Chester, Exeter, Norwich and York. The initial letters of these mints appear on the half-crowns, shillings and sixpences of 1696–97 (William III).

The final union between England and Scotland took place in 1707, and between 1707 and 1709 an 'E' or an 'E' with a star occurs on such silver coins as were struck at the Edinburgh mint. Before this time and until the reign of George I Scotland continued to have its own denominations and designs for coins. The last coins actually struck for Scotland were in 1709, after which the Edinburgh mint seems to have ceased production completely. The office of Governor of the Mint of Scotland was not formally abolished till 1817.

One other mark appears on the last shillings and sixpences struck in Scotland, that of a small star, which occurs between 1707 and 1709. Its purpose is not definitely known, but it is thought to represent either supplementary issues or that the pieces so marked were struck from metal which had been called in.

Though machines had been introduced variety did not disappear from the coinage. In most reigns various busts were used at different periods, generally showing the king or queen getting older. In other cases busts were redesigned to give a more acceptable appearance.

Reverse designs also varied somewhat, though the most common type is that of four shields placed cruciform, somewhat similar to the readoption of this design on the crowns of 1953. In the gold coins there are often two sceptres in saltire, and on many denominations the initial letters of the monarch's name are used as decorations, together with the letters and symbols referred to above.

In spite of machinery, mistakes occasionally slipped past the eagle eyes of the Mint authorities and still do. Recently some crowns of 1953 have been seen on which the edge legend is incomplete, due apparently to the misplacing or fracture of the collar, while at least two shillings with the head of Queen Elizabeth on both sides have been recorded. Brockages, that is coins with the obverse or reverse design in relief on one side and incuse on the other, sometimes appear, as do coins the flans of which have spread due to the absence or fracture of the collar. Such coins are few, since every coin is examined before it leaves the Mint. Such mis-struck coins do not generally excite the collector. To him they are not a true representation of the coin they purport to be. A misprinted stamp sells for a considerable sum; a mis-struck coin creates less interest.

The first big difference in what had become the established design of milled coins occurred in the reign of William and Mary. Since they reigned as joint monarchs both their heads appeared on the coins, side by side. The reverses of some denominations contained one large shield of arms, somewhat similar to the present half-crowns. On others the date was placed in a somewhat confusing circular position in the centre of the coin reverse.

With the introduction of milled coins began the custom of turning the head of each succeeding monarch in the opposite direction to that of his predecessor. Charles II is said to have deliberately caused his head to be represented on his coins so that his back was turned in contempt on his predecessor, Cromwell. James II (1685–88) faced in the opposite direction to his predecessor, his brother Charles II, and in this way the custom seems to have been established. It was not till the short reign of Edward VIII that a break would have been made. Such very few coins, twelve-sided threepences, as succeeded in getting out of the Royal Mint and of eluding subsequent recapture, show Edward VIII facing in the same direction as his father, George V. Some reference is made to this in the memoirs written by the King as Duke of Windsor (p. 294). With the accession of George VI the Royal Mint proceeded as though custom had been adhered to, that is as though Edward VIII had faced right. They were apparently unaware that, apart from a set of coins in the Royal collection, a very few threepences had reached the hands of collectors. George VI therefore faced to the left, thus giving three kings in succession, George V, Edward VIII and George VI, who have all faced left. With the reign of Elizabeth II tradition has again prevailed.

Thus briefly the milled issues from 1662 to 1816. They are fully documented and illustrated in publications devoted entirely to this section of the English coinage. With the Napoleonic wars, the coming of steam-power and the experiments and persistence of Messrs Boulton and Watt, a further considerable change again came upon the coinage giving it the form which has survived till the present.

The period of the reign of George III (1760–1820) saw many events of great historical importance, affecting the coinage in various ways. The issue of coins between the years 1760 and 1816 consisted almost entirely of guineas. The five- and two-guinea pieces, though prepared as patterns, were not struck for circulation and do not appear in the English series again. Guineas and half-guineas were coined with six or seven different types of obverse and the third of a guinea appeared as a new denomination, to disappear again on the reform of the coinage. So far as coinage was concerned the sovereign still included the French title in the legend, though Calais, England's last French possession, had been lost in the reign of Mary I.

This was the period of the well-known 'spade guinea', so called on account of the shape of the shield of arms on the reverse. This is the coin which has proved so popular with the writers of certain types of fiction, who delight in its use in highwayman stories. In actual fact, by the time the 'spade guinea' appeared (1787), the highwaymen had been almost swept from the roads, which were beginning that stage of development which offered reasonably safe transit, made coach travelling the rule rather than the exception, and placed England in the forefront of road travel over all the countries of Europe.

Though it may be somewhat unexpected, the period 1760–1816 saw the silver currency almost completely neglected. From 1760 till 1787 the only silver coins to be issued were shillings in 1763, and Maundy money. These shillings were to become known as 'Northumberland shillings', as they were struck for distribution by the Earl of Northumberland at his entry into Dublin as Lord-Lieutenant of Ireland. In 1787 large quantities of shillings and sixpences were minted and from the fact that they so frequently appear today in mint state it would seem that they must largely have been kept as souvenirs.

This absence of a proper provision for silver coin was to be remedied in an unexpected way. In 1797, the extraordinary expedient was resorted to of issuing Spanish eight-real pieces, or 'Spanish dollars' as they were known, and of which there were vast quantities about, overstamped with the head of George III. The countermark was small and oval, usually on the neck of the King of Spain. This gave rise to the saying that the coins portrayed 'the head of a fool on the neck of an ass'. In 1804 this stamp was changed for a larger, octagonal in shape and similar to that used on the silver penny as regards the countermark of the king's head.

These countermarked pieces were declared current at 4*s*. 9*d*., thus giving rise to the saying that 'two king's heads were not worth a crown'. By one of those governmental oversights which sometimes occur, the silver content of the pieces was more than the face value of the coin. There was a rush to sell them as bullion, and many forgeries of the coins were manufactured. Subdivisions of the Spanish eight-real pieces are also said to have been similarly countermarked and they not infrequently appear today. Of late years some doubt has been thrown upon their authenticity, since documentary evidence for their issue appears to be lacking.

The financial muddle that resulted from the foregoing can well be imagined. In an attempt to straighten things out, the Bank of England obtained in 1804 permission to issue a dollar, to be current at 5*s*., and this permission was extended in 1811 to cover also coins of the value of three shillings and of one shilling and sixpence. This is the only occasion on which the dollar formed part of the official currency of Britain. At a later date a British dollar was struck for use in Malaya and the Far East and another for Hong Kong, but these were never current in the British Isles.

The Bank of England dollar was made from the long-suffering Spanish eight-real piece by the removal of the original devices from the surface and the restamping of the flan with the approved Bank of England design. In some cases parts of the original lettering or design can still be seen below the new striking. The eight-real piece, by reason of its profusion, was often selected for overstriking, restriking, countermarking, cutting into sections, and for general mutilation by any and every country short of specie. The early coinages of the West Indies and of Australia have many examples of this coin used in various forms. The history of the piece has been recently written in a four-volume work, published in Spain, and the size of such a treatise on one particular coin will give some idea of the multifarious uses to which this piece has been put.

Dies were also prepared for the striking of pieces to circulate at 5*s*. 6*d*. and 9*d*., but none of the former and only a few of the latter ever circulated. A series of pattern dollars, mostly very scarce pieces, was struck before the final design was approved or as suggested alternative types to the approved design. A few dollars were also struck in gold as patterns. These are extremely rare, and it is possible that they are not all contemporary. Their appearance always creates considerable interest among collectors, and in recent years one of them realised at auction the highest price ever recorded up to that time for any English coin.

Obviously such a state of the coinage could not be allowed to continue for very long. After much argument on the subject, the Royal Mint moved from its traditional home in the Tower of London, where it had been from time immemorial. The new Royal Mint on Tower Hill was equipped by Boulton and Watt, about whom something has already been said in these pages. The equipment which they installed was then the finest in the world, and produced accurate coins for weight and shape.

With the new coinage began the range of denominations as we know them today. The sovereign was the unit, with five-pound and two-pound pieces appearing in subsequent reigns. Half-sovereigns were the only other gold coins. Crowns, half-crowns, shillings and sixpences were standardised as the silver coins for general circulation with the 4*d.* (groat), 3*d.*, 2*d.* (half-groat) and 1*d.* issued in silver for the Royal Maundy money. Later the threepence also went into general circulation, continuing in use till 1946, when strikings, apart from Maundy money, were suspended in favour of the twelve-sided threepence.

This also is the period in which the modern conception of St. George and the Dragon appeared on coins, its use being restricted to the sovereign and half-sovereign, the five-pounds, the two-pounds and the crown, on all of which it has appeared at various times. An interesting story told in Forrer's *Biographical Dictionary of Medallists* lies behind its adoption.

The design as adopted was made by Benedetto Pistrucci (1784–1855), an Italian medallist and gem engraver. He arrived in London about 1814, when the design of the new coinage was the subject of considerable suggestion and argument, and he put up at Brunet's Hotel, in Leicester Square.

'The Italian artist having suggested St. George and the Dragon as a suitable subject for the reverse of the new gold coinage, he was commissioned by Pole to execute a cameo of it in jasper, to be copied; for which he paid him, by agreement, one hundred guineas. At this juncture (1817) T. Wyon died and from the ill-success of the copy of Pistrucci's George III by the Mint-engraver, and the improbability of any other person in the Mint being able to copy the George and Dragon, the Master considered that it would be necessary to employ Pistrucci himself to engrave both subjects on the dies, and offered him the post of Chief-engraver, with a salary of five hundred pounds per annum, and one of the houses within the walls of the Royal Mint appropriated for the officers of the establishment.*

'The jasper George and the Dragon, purchased by Wellesley Pole for the coins, was an *original*, and not the cameo, or wax model, which he had made previously for a "George" to be worn by Earl Spencer, K.G. The design was considerably modified, and the St. George was modelled from life, the original being an Italian servant in Brunet's Hotel.

'Pistrucci's St. George and the Dragon first appeared on the Sovereign of 1817 and Pattern Crowns of the same date. The Crown of George IV was called by Denon, the Director of the French Mint, the handsomest coin in Europe.

'"The design, still retained, does not," observes Mr. Wroth, "strictly speaking, owe its origin to Pistrucci. It can be traced back to a shell-cameo, the 'Bataille coquille,' in the collection of the Duke of Orleans. This was copied, at least in part, by Giovanni Pichler, whose intaglio with this subject became popular in Rome. Pistrucci himself, when in Italy, had made four copies (two cameos and two intaglios) of Pichler's intaglio."

'Referring to the reverse of the Crown, Hawkins criticises the design. "The position of the right leg was purposely, but unfortunately, changed: for, as the hero now sits upon his horse, he must inevitably fall to the ground the moment he attempts to strike the meditated blow with the sword." In answer to this criticism, Billing remarks: "Now Pistrucci, who had doated upon horses from his childhood and who – as was said of Murat, and perhaps of many others – 'rode like a Centaur', was not likely to represent a hero that could not keep his seat: on the contrary, everyone can see on the Sovereign, Double-Sovereign, or Crown piece, that the rider sits perfectly straight and firm – that the left foot is visible below the horse's belly, showing that the rider has closed his *left* leg to counterbalance the exertion of the *right* arm."'

Such a story is typical of many that could be told about various designs that have been used on English coins down the ages. The last use to date of the St. George and Dragon

* The appointment was never confirmed as, under an Act of William III (1694–1702), no foreigner could hold a position of trust at the Royal Mint. And so began 38 years of trouble with Pistrucci.

motif was on the crown of 1951 and on the present issues of sovereigns where the points raised in the above controversy can be studied.

The new coinage was a considerable departure from what had become traditional in English coin design. No doubt it had its critics, but, whatever its artistic merits, one thing at least can be said of it which is not true of the first coinage of the present reign: in execution it was excellent.

It is not, apparently, generally known that all English silver coins struck since 1816 are still current and legal tender.

The reign of George III saw the introduction of the copper range of penny, halfpenny and farthing in the form in which we know them today. At this time and until 1860 these three pieces were struck in pure copper; the present bronze coinage, smaller in size and thinner, was introduced in that year. In 1797 Boulton began to strike the copper coinage on behalf of the Government. In the first year a twopenny-piece was struck, but this continued for 1797 only. The coins were large and heavy, just over 1½ inches in diameter and weighing two ounces avoirdupois. So accurate were they in this respect that they were occasionally used as two-ounce weights. They had a broad rim, raised, on which was an incuse legend, and the rim and their size earned for them the name of 'cartwheel twopence'. This description and type of coin was also applied to the penny, which weighed one ounce. After undergoing some revision as regards design the penny continued, with the halfpenny and farthing added, and these three denominations continued to be struck at Birmingham for a number of years. At intervals Boulton and Watt and their successors have received contracts for the striking of copper coinage until quite recent years. The products of their successors are often marked with an 'H' (Heaton & Company) by way of privy mark. This continues a practice which started at this period, and which included the striking of the minor denominations of the coinage for various Colonies and Protectorates. One of the latest pieces to appear from this source is the revived Hong Kong Dollar, to which further reference is made in Chapter Nine.

After some redesigning the range of coinage now established continued into the reign of George IV (1820–30), with the double sovereign or two-pound piece making its appearance in 1823. Patterns were prepared for the five-pound piece, but it did not appear as a general issue. These five- and two-pound pieces have never appeared in large numbers in general circulation, though the denominations have been perpetuated in the form of patterns and proofs and as collector's pieces till 1937. No doubt they were also struck as proofs in the very limited issues of gold coins which are believed to have been struck to keep the gold denominations alive during the present reign.

These two large gold coins again only appeared as patterns during the reign of William IV (1830–37), though the larger is perhaps only the crown struck in gold. For circulation only the sovereigns and half-sovereigns were struck. Nor did the silver crown appear in this reign except in the form of a proof. At the suggestion of Joseph Hume a groat or fourpenny-piece, apart from the Maundy fourpence, made its appearance in 1836. This was a charming coin, with the seated figure of Britannia on the reverse. From its originator the piece received the familiar name of a 'Joey', and was continued into the next reign until 1856. It is said to owe its origin to the fact that Sir Joseph once tipped a cabby half a sovereign in mistake for a sixpence.

6. VICTORIA TO ELIZABETH II

The long reign of Victoria (1837–1901) saw many changes in the modelling of the coinage. The first series has become known as the 'young head' type, showing the Queen as an attractive young woman, executed with a fineness of line which the modern coins would do well to emulate. In this first series all denominations were issued up to the sovereign, but not every denomination appeared in each succeeding year. This had, however, pertained through many previous reigns. A very handsome five-pound piece was prepared, showing the Queen as Una, leading the British Lion, but unfortunately this coin never appeared in circulation, nor was it struck in any considerable numbers. By some it was thought to be too medallic in its presentation; but it was a fine piece, and is a desirable rarity among collectors today who specialise in gold coins.

In 1849 an entirely new denomination appeared, the silver florin. This was minted as a result of persistent agitation that the coinage should be put on a decimal basis. Only this one denomination ever appeared, as a tenth of a pound, though various patterns of coins on a decimal system were prepared.

The florin showed on its obverse the Queen wearing an elaborate crown and the legend VICTORIA REGINA, together with the date. The absence of the words DEI GRATIA, or the letters D.G. (by the grace of God), soon earned for the coin the name of 'godless florin'. The reverse had cruciform shields of arms, interspaced with national emblems, and the whole design reflected the Gothic revival of the times, a revival which saw such buildings erected as the Houses of Parliament, St. Pancras Station, and the Law Courts.

In 1851 the coin was redesigned, still on Gothic lines and on a slightly larger flan. A long series of these handsome 'Gothic florins' appeared, the range continuing till 1887. For some twenty years no half-crowns were struck, since the florin was thought to meet the requirements. The DEI GRATIA was restored to the legend and the coin was dated in Roman numerals. This often gives rise to the mistaken idea that the coin is undated when it appears, as it still occasionally does, in circulation.

Plate 19 ENGLISH COINS: ELIZABETH II, JAMES I, A XVII CENTURY TOKEN

81. Coronation Crown, in cupro-nickel, of Elizabeth II. The mounted figure and cruciform shields show a reversion to the influence of earlier times.
82. The only silver coins left in circulation: a set of Maundy Money, 1953. Though legal tender these coins pass among collectors at a considerable premium.
83. A copper Harington Farthing. The result of the agitation for a copper coinage.
84. A typical copper seventeenth-century Token. Issued by a London trader, this piece, typical of thousands, was the people's answer to the absence of small change.

Plate 19

85
LONDON PROMISSORY PENNY TOKEN
86
CAROLUS·IIII·DEI·GRATIA·1808
4|6
GREENOCK
HISPAN·ET·IND·REX·M·8R·T·F·
87
ELIZABETH II DEI GRATIA REGINA
CANADA
1953
DOLLAR

A very handsome 'Gothic crown' was also struck, on the same general lines of design. These pieces are often considered to be the most handsome coins ever struck among the modern series. Certainly the workmanship was of the highest order and the design was crowded with minute detail.

In 1887 the coinage was redesigned in celebration of the Queen's Jubilee. The obverse carried a bust of the Queen, now much older, with a tiny crown perched precariously on the top of her veiled head. This design was so unpopular that its immediate revision was called for, and this was undertaken in 1893. The little crown may be seen among the Crown Jewels at the Tower.

For the 1887 Jubilee a number of specimen sets of coins were struck both as proofs and as ordinary coins. These sets contained the five- and two-pound pieces. These two denominations were not intended for circulation and were made from gold purchased by the Mint for the purpose. In so far as any non-pattern coins struck by the Royal Mint are *prima facie* legal tender these pieces could circulate, but it is doubtful if many of them did.

The redesigned coinage of 1893, often called the 'old head' type, was also issued in specimen sets as well as for general circulation. Again the sets were of both proof and ordinary pieces,

Plate 20 ENGLISH TOKENS AND COMMONWEALTH COINS

85. Copper nineteenth-century Token. Issued by a London trader, from Boulton and Watt's mint in Birmingham, this piece, typical of a large series, shows a contemporary view of the Mansion House.
86. An example of the long-suffering silver Spanish Eight Reales piece, privately countermarked to serve as token currency in Greenock. In local circulation it passed at 4s. 6d.
87. A silver Dollar of the Dominion of Canada, struck at the Ottawa Mint.

with the same proviso in respect of the five-and two-pound pieces. Both obverse and reverse were redesigned, the former showing the Queen as an old lady with veiled head, and the latter depicting a variety of the traditional heraldic scheme.

Until 1860 copper pennies, halfpennies and farthings were issued. These handsome pieces, of the 'young head' type, were somewhat larger in size than those of the present series. In that year the bronze 'bun' penny, with the halfpenny and farthing in the same metal, appeared, thus commencing the bronze minor issues with which we are now familiar. Bronze coins from 1860 onwards are still legal tender.

A very handsome design of obverse was prepared by the artist William Wyon, celebrated in his day for his fine numismatic work. With Pistrucci the Wyon family designed probably the most successful numismatic material ever struck by the mechanical process.

The little 'Britannia groat' appeared for a few years during the reign but was eventually discontinued. It lingered on as a colonial coin, in a redesigned form, until recent times, while the Maundy groat continued in uninterrupted sequence year by year.

There remains little to be added about what are now the everyday coins. New designs were introduced for Edward VII (1901–10), and again specimen sets from the five-pound piece downwards through the gold and silver denominations were struck, this time to mark the Coronation. Probably the most pleasing coin of the new reign was the florin, on the reverse of which was the standing figure of Britannia.

Further new designs were introduced for the reign of George V (1910–36), some being little more than modifications of the designs of the previous reign. Specimen sets of proof coins, now an established feature, were struck to mark the Coronation, but no crown appeared. This large silver piece had almost disappeared from circulation after the reign of Victoria, and a foolish legend had grown up to the effect that as a coin it was an unlucky piece. Had it not been for pressure brought to bear by numismatists and other interested parties, it seems likely that this coin would have silently disappeared from the range.

Hearing that the coinage was to be remodelled in 1927 action was taken, with the result that when the new coins appeared and a specimen set of silver pieces was issued to introduce the new designs, the crown once more came on the scene. With the exception of 1935, the year of the Jubilee of George V when many crowns were struck, the piece was issued in very small numbers during this reign. The normal issue had an emblematic wreath and crown as the reverse design, but this was changed for the year 1935 only, when St. George and the Dragon again appeared, but in a highly modernistic form resembling a mechanical robot.

During the First World War the sovereign and half-sovereign disappeared from circulation not to appear again, so far, as an everyday coin. They retained Pistrucci's St. George and the Dragon on the reverse. Debasement of the silver content of the coinage took place during the reign as an aftermath of the war and for a time coins of very poor alloy were issued. These soon showed a coppery appearance. The alloy was later improved, though many of the poorer specimens are still available.

Remodelling and some new designs appeared in 1937 to introduce the coinage of George VI (1936–52). Specimen sets of proof coins were struck, the four gold coins making a token appearance in this year only. No gold coins were struck for circulation during the reign.

Two new coins appeared. One was the Scottish shilling, issued each year during the reign in about equal numbers with the English shilling. This coin was not intended for sole circulation in Scotland, but as a compliment to the Queen Consort and her Scottish ancestry.

The second coin, the twelve-sided threepence, a revised version of that struck for Edward VIII but not circulated, was entirely new to the public, first appearing in 1937. By many it was scorned, especially in Scotland, but it lived to prove its use, particularly in the blackout of the Second World War, when its size and shape made it readily recognisable. By 1946, when silver coins were discontinued in favour of cupro-nickel, the new threepence was an accepted coin, and had 'killed' its silver counterpart, which was no longer struck except in the Maundy series. The crown appeared in 1937, both as a proof and as an ordinary coin, this time having the Royal Arms on the reverse.

Apart from a few minor colonial coins, bearing no portrait, no coins were issued during the short reign of Edward VIII (1936). A very few proofs were struck, a set being included in the Royal Collection at Windsor Castle. As already mentioned a few of the twelve-sided threepences, then in preparation, did succeed in getting out of the Mint and not being returned. Various reasons are assigned to this, the most likely being that a number were struck in advance and lent to the makers of automatic ticket machines to test the coin's usefulness for this purpose and to allow machines to be adjusted to take the new coin. They are considered of great rarity, and their reverse design, similar to that eventually adopted in 1937, was of a more pleasing appearance.

Since George V died in January 1936, those coins which were issued in that year, bearing his head and titles, are by some considered to have been issued by Edward VIII, and to constitute the coin issues of his short reign. This may be academically true, but there is not very much satisfaction to be obtained by the collector in so referring to these particular coins. It is as true to say that coins issued in 1952, after the death in February of George VI, are the first issue of Elizabeth II but bearing her father's head and titles. As has been already indicated, there is always an overrun of this type at the end of a reign, and it is not customary for the coins of a new reign to appear more than a few days before the Coronation, which cannot take place for at least one year after the death of the former sovereign (but compare pp. 74 and 75).

For the first time since it had become the custom to issue specimen sets to mark the new reign, no gold coins were included when such sets appeared in 1953. The coins, being of cupro-nickel, presented more difficulty in preparation, one of the excuses offered subsequently for their poor execution. Maundy money alone survived the change from silver in 1946 and continued to be issued in this metal.

The 400th anniversary, which coincided with the centenary of the Great Exhibition of 1851, was marked by the issue of a cupro-nickel crown in 1951, with the familiar St. George and the Dragon reverse, the design reverting to the form introduced by Pistrucci. For the first time for many centuries some of these coins were struck outside the walls of the Royal Mint, at a special branch mint set up for the purpose on the Festival site. The only parallel in modern times is that of a special branch mint established in a country area as a precaution during the Second World War, but its issues were not prolific, and cannot be distinguished.

As previously stated, the Coronation crown of Elizabeth II returned to a fine old precedent, the obverse design showing the Queen on horseback. This design, though poorly executed when compared with the crowns of 1551, was immensely popular, some 5,000,000 specimens being struck and rapidly taken up by the public. A second design for future use was also prepared, and was used for the crown struck in 1960.

Considerable redesigning took place with both the obverse and reverse of all the coins for the new reign. The legend on the obverse returned to a continuous circle, unbroken by the bust of the Sovereign. For the first time a woman was responsible for the obverse design, that of a bust instead of the familiar truncated head which appeared with the new coinage of 1816. Though happy in conception the new design, in contrast with the bust of Victoria by Wyon, is in such low relief that parts of it are indistinct even on uncirculated specimens.

The reverses of the coins were completely redesigned, and here the designers, of which there were several, were rather more successful in their presentation of arms and traditional emblems which were, apparently, within the capacity of the Mint to strike with reasonably good execution. The Coronation crown appeared with cruciform shields on the reverse and the remaining designs are now familiar to us all. Perhaps one of the most pleasing was that of the twelve-sided threepence, where the Tudor portcullis made an unexpected reappearance. The design of the reverse of the florin was not quite so successful. Its appearance is so complicated that in illustrating the piece on its introduction only a few of the daily newspapers succeeded in showing the piece the correct way round.

CHAPTER SEVEN

Maundy Money

AN ANCIENT ROYAL CEREMONY

THROUGHOUT these pages reference has been made at intervals to Maundy money. The coins associated with this title consist today of silver penny, twopence, threepence and fourpence, and are the only silver coins now left in the English series.

The ceremony of the Royal Maundy goes back so far into antiquity that its origins have long been lost. A ceremony of this nature takes place not only in England but in several others in Europe. It is said to be derived from the *Mandatum* which Our Lord delivered to His Disciples the day before He was crucified. At the same time the act of washing His Disciples' feet became a part of the original ceremony.

In its early form the Sovereign or the Royal Almoner washed the feet of a number of poor people, distributed to them food and clothing and money. In detail the ceremony, held on Maundy Thursday, has changed from time to time. The number of poor persons has altered, the distribution of clothing or cloth and food, either in the form of an actual distribution of articles, or of a meal served as part of the ceremony, have all been altered or adapted as time went on, but a distribution of money seems always to have formed a part of the ceremony.

During the centuries that have passed the ceremony has been held in various places. In 1572 Queen Elizabeth I took part personally in the ceremony, which was held in the Hall at Greenwich, then a town outside the boundary of Tudor London.

The following account of the ceremony is taken from a book entitled *The Royal Maundy* by Mr. E. E. Ratcliffe, M.V.O., sometime Assistant Secretary of the Royal Almonry:

'A cushion was placed in front of each person for the Queen to kneel upon, and her chaplain conducted the service. First the laundress, who was provided with a silver basin containing warm water and sweet flowers, washed the feet of the poor people, and then, after the singing of a hymn, the Sub-Almoner and the Lord High Almoner in turn repeated the process. The chaplain read the lesson describing the washing of the Disciples' feet, and then the Queen entered the Hall, attended by thirty-nine ladies and gentlemen, the number corresponding to the years of Her Majesty's age. The "gentlefolks" put on aprons, and bearing towels and basins of water and sweet flowers, waited on the Queen, who washed, crossed and kissed the feet of the poor women, as the laundress, the Sub-Almoner and the Lord High Almoner had done before her. She then distributed the presents: broadcloth with which to make gowns, a pair of sleeves, a wooden platter upon which was half a side of salmon, the same amount of ling, six red herrings, and six loaves of "cheat-bread", together with a white wooden dish of claret wine. She also bestowed on the poor women the towels she had used and the aprons worn by the attendants. The long ceremonial was then at an end, and the Queen took her departure. "By this time the sun was setting", pithily remarks the old chronicler to whom we are indebted for this record.'

This was the ceremony as fully carried out at this time. It was not always so considerable, nor did the Sovereign always attend in person. At one time others besides the Sovereign gave Maundy doles. Wolsey and other great prelates and noblemen did so, but in such cases it was usual for the number of recipients to be limited to twelve, representing the Apostles.

In the reign of Charles I, during the Civil War, the ceremony was held at York in 1639, when it was carried out 'for the King' in York Minster. It was again held at York in 1642.

On some occasions, owing to outbreaks of the Plague, the King refrained from performing the ceremony of washing the feet, but Charles II resumed it in spite of this danger. The last time on which this rite was performed was in 1685.

One change of note was made in 1724, when the women received a payment of money in lieu of clothing. This was done because many of them were so anxious to try the clothing for size that they could not refrain from doing so during the ceremony.

For many years the ceremony was held in Whitehall Chapel, but was moved from here in 1890.

Various other detailed changes took place as time went on. In 1837 William IV agreed that the sum of thirty shillings should be paid to the recipients in lieu of provisions, since it was found that these were often sold by the recipients for a mere trifle, having cost the Crown thirty shillings per head. In 1882 an allowance of money was made to the men in lieu of clothing. By this time cloth rather than actual garments was being distributed, and it was found that many were too poor to be able to afford to have the cloth made up by a tailor into clothes.

In the time when the silver penny, half-groat, threepence and groat formed a part of the everyday currency, these were used, at any rate in part, to make up the actual money given as a part of the Maundy distribution. As time passed and these coins began to fall out of everyday use, they were minted specially for this purpose. Even before this time there are records of a special amount of silver being set aside for the purpose of coining sufficient of these four coins to meet the demands created by the Maundy distribution.

Collectors of Maundy money have for many years considered that these four coins could be regarded as Maundy money from the reign of Charles II. Brooke, however, states:

'The common belief that the sixpence was the lowest denomination now (1662) struck for ordinary currency, and that the smaller coins were made for Maundy distribution, is incorrect. The penny, which was the only coin distributed as Maundy, was struck under ordinary indenture and circulated. It was not till 1729, or possibly 1731, that the pieces of 4*d*., 3*d*., and 2*d*., were used as Maundy, and only since that date have they and the silver penny ceased to circulate as currency. Maundy money is, of course, and always has been, legal tender. The term "Maundy Money" is only applicable in and after the reign of George II.'

It will be appreciated that, since the total value of the four coins is ten pence, it forms an easy multiple from which to work in placing in each Maundy purse the number of pence corresponding to the years of the Sovereign's age.

From the reign of James II until 1935 the Sovereign did not

attend the ceremony in person. In that year, the Jubilee of King George V, the King and Queen Mary attended the ceremony, the King personally handing the gifts to the recipients. The money is contained in traditional red and white leather purses. King Edward VIII, in 1936, followed the example of his father in distributing the gifts in person, and this happy tradition was again revived and was continued by George VI in 1940, 1944, 1945, 1946, 1948, 1950 and 1951. So far it has been continued by Queen Elizabeth II, though in 1954 she was unable to attend the ceremony as she was visiting her Dominions and Colonies, while in 1960 the birth of Prince Andrew prevented her attendance in person; the distribution was then made by Queen Elizabeth, the Queen Mother. In 1964 the late Princess Royal made the distribution on behalf of the Queen.

For a short account of the historic ceremony as it is now performed, the following is quoted from the book already mentioned:

'The Royal Maundy Ceremony now takes place in Westminster Abbey, and though shorn of some of its original features, still bears a resemblance to the service used in Queen Elizabeth's time. It is one of the few occasions when the public sees the King's Bodyguard of the Yeomen of the Guard in their full uniform. This is the oldest military body in the kingdom, whose record dates back to 1485 and who still wear, with proud distinction, the Tudor crown ornament which commemorates their original appointment.

'Although the washing of feet was discontinued in the seventeenth century, all the Almonry officials continue to be girt with towels and carry the traditional nosegays. Prior to the year 1908 there were entered on the Almonry Records the names of some old men who were called the Children of the Royal Almonry. Their duties were to attend at the Chapel Royal on Maundy Thursday arrayed in linen scarves. Their fees in the aggregate amounted to £21 for this service. This being considered an abuse of the Charity these old men were pensioned off and a new class of "children" instituted. These are children in reality, generally selected from the families of deceased officers of the three Services and appointed as Children of the Almonry. To these children a grant for aiding their education is made. They do not attend the ceremony personally, but are represented by four children selected from the schools of the parishes of St. John the Evangelist with St. Stephen and St. Margaret, Westminster.

'The Royal Full Maundy as it now exists is made up as follows, the amounts quoted being for male recipients:

'In a red leather purse with white thongs:

	£	s.	d.
(1) For the redemption of the Sovereign's gown worn on the day of Distribution	£1	0	0
(2) Allowance in lieu of provisions	£1	10	0
'In a white leather purse with red thongs:			
The number of pence, according to the age of the reigning Sovereign, in silver coins, specially struck for the occasion by the Royal Mint, and consisting (in 1951) of five penny, six twopenny, five threepenny and six fourpenny, pieces, amounting this year to	£0	4	8
'In a white leather purse with green thongs:			
Allowance in lieu of clothing	£2	5	0
Total	£4	19	8

'Women receive £4 9*s*. 8*d*., their clothing allowance being £1 15*s*. in a green purse.

'Recipients are chosen from among those applying to the Royal Almonry for assistance, preference being given to those who have formerly been householders paying rates and taxes and who have been employers of labour.

'With the assistance of four "Wandsmen" (each carries a "Staff" or "Wand"), those who are to receive the Maundy Gifts, and who are able to be present at the service, are seated on either side of the Choir and in the Nave.

'The procession forms in the Nave of the Abbey. Their Majesties The King and Queen, when attending, are met at the West Door by the Dean of Westminster, and are presented with nosegays of sweet herbs in accordance with ancient custom. During the singing of the hymn "Praise My Soul the King of Heaven" the procession passes from the Nave into the Choir.

'Their Majesties The King and Queen, the Dean, the Lord High Almoner, the Sub-Almoner, the Secretary, Assistant Secretary, and the Abbey Clergy proceed to the Sanctuary.

'The Alms Dishes with the Purses, carried by Yeomen in the procession, are placed on tables at the foot of the steps leading to the Sanctuary.

'The silver gilt dish with the red and white purses is carried in the procession on the head of a Yeoman. This dish was given by Charles II and is kept, except on this day, among the Regalia at the Tower of London.

'H.M.'s Bodyguard of the Yeomen of the Guard are on duty in the Nave and Choir, and the Yeomen deputed to carry the dishes during the actual distribution take up their positions behind the tables upon which the Alms Dishes have been placed.

'On the steps of the Sanctuary, in the presence of Their Majesties The King and Queen, and the high dignitaries of Church and State, sit the four representatives of the Children of the Royal Almonry – two boys on the right and two girls on the left.

'The Precentor reads the Prayers, and the Minor Canon Appearer the lessons.

'The Service opens with the Exhortation from St. John, xiii, 34: "A new Commandment have I given unto you, that ye love one another; as I have loved you, that ye also love one another." Hilton's anthem "Lord, for thy tender mercies' sake," follows the singing of Psalm XCI.

'At the end of the First Lesson, St. John, xiii, 1–16, and while Wesley's anthem, "Wash me thoroughly from my wickedness," is being sung, the First Distribution takes place. This consists of a money gift of £2 5*s*. in lieu of clothing in a white purse to each man, and £1 15*s*. in a green purse to each woman.

'The Distribution procedure is as follows: The Secretary and the Assistant Secretary girt with towels first take up their positions by the table. The Yeoman removes the Alms Dish and carries it throughout the Distribution.

'The Lord High Almoner and the Sub-Almoner, in their

surplices and girt with towels, preceded by the Dean's Verger, conduct the King to the foot of the steps leading to the Sanctuary.

'The Assistant Secretary takes the purses from the Dish and hands them to the Sub-Almoner. He passes them to the Lord High Almoner, who hands them to the King. His Majesty then hands the purses to each recipient indicated by the Secretary who precedes the King.

'In making the Distribution H.M. the King and the Lord High Almoner, with their Assistants, pass down the Choir and into the Nave, handing the gifts first to the women, who are placed on the south side, and then, as they return, to the men, who are placed on the north side.

'At the end of the Second Lesson, St. Matthew, xxv, 31 to the end, and during the singing of the anthems "If ye love me, keep my commandments" (Tallis), and "Zadok the Priest" (Handel), the Second Distribution of red and white purses takes place. These purses are tied together by their strings. The white contains Maundy money in penny, twopenny, threepenny and fourpenny pieces, in amount equivalent to the years of the King's age, and the red a gift of £2 10*s*. – being £1 10*s*. in lieu of Provisions and £1 Redemption Money. . . .

'The procedure for this Distribution follows that of the First Distribution.

'The General Thanksgiving is said "by the priest and people, all devoutly kneeling", followed by the singing of the "Old Hundredth".

'The Blessing is given by the Dean of Westminster, and the Service concludes with the singing of the National Anthem.'

It will be appreciated that the above account relates to a Distribution by the late King, but the same will apply in the present reign. It is one of those ancient ceremonies filled with colour and pageantry for which the kingdom with its long history is justly famed, and the special Maundy coins, the only silver coins now left in the series, form the central point around which the whole of the ceremony pivots. A limited number of tickets to attend the ceremony are available to the public, who should apply in writing to the Royal Almonry, Buckingham Palace.

In recent years the ceremony has taken place in churches other than Westminster Abbey. It was held in St. Paul's Cathedral in 1953, Southwark Cathedral in 1955, St. Albans Cathedral in 1957, St. George's Chapel, Windsor Castle, in 1959, Rochester Cathedral in 1961, Chelmsford in 1963 and Canterbury in 1965.

CHAPTER EIGHT

Tokens: The Coinage of the People

IN DEALING with the subject of copper and bronze coinage reference has been made to tokens. It will be remembered that as economic values gradually rose, the need for some kind of minor currency became apparent. In the age of the silver penny, the question was answered for a time by cutting these coins into halves and quarters, leading in due course to the appearance of the round halfpenny and the farthing.

These methods served their purpose for a time, but as the centuries passed the need repeated itself, and considerable hardship was eventually caused by the absence of a suitable minor coinage to meet public needs. Finally, in the sixteenth century shopkeepers began to issue token pieces in lead and tin. In reply, the Government of the day (*circa* 1576), after considering a copper coinage of halfpence and farthings, patterns for which appeared, drafted a proclamation, which is undated and was probably never issued, prohibiting the tokens and legalising a limited tender of halfpenny and farthing 'pledges' made of pure copper. These attempts to stop the issue of tokens were not successful.

In his complete *Catalogue of English Copper, Tin and Bronze Coins in the British Museum, 1858–1958*, compiled after many years of study, Mr. Wilson Peck gives the following account of the minor coinage position in the reign of James I (1603–1625).

'Several proposals for coining copper tokens were considered during the period 1607–12, but despite the fact that James I well knew the advantages which had resulted from the issue of copper pieces in Scotland, nothing was done until he ultimately "conceived the unhappy idea of placing the issue of such money in the hands of private persons" who, as holders of the monopoly, could be heavily charged for the privilege and yield him, so it was estimated, a profit of £25,000. The plan was finally drawn up on 10 April 1613 and set out in a proclamation dated 19 May, 1613.

'This commenced with an admission that there had been "some toleration" in the past of leaden tokens which were used as small change between traders and their customers, "whereby such small portions and quantities of things vendible . . . may be conveniently bought and sold without enforcing men to buy more ware than will serve for their use and occasions".

'It objected, however, to the manner in which these tokens were issued; that they were subject to counterfeiting and in consequence were sometimes refused as "doubtful things"; that they were often discredited after the death of those who had issued them; and, finally, that it was derogatory to the royal prerogative that such tokens should be allowed currency with the lawful money of the realm.

'It went on to explain that the king, recognising the need for such small moneys, had given power and authority, by letters patent, to John, Lord Harington of Exton, to issue sufficient copper farthing tokens for use within the realms of England and Ireland and the dominion of Wales, for a period of three years and that they were "to pass for the value of farthings . . . with the liking and consent of his loving subjects". In other words, they were not coin of the realm and could not be forced as legal tender; they were, in fact, intended solely for the convenience of any who chose to use them.

'The proclamation also ordered that "the said farthings should be made exactly and artificially of copper, by engines and instruments, having on the one side two sceptres crossing under one diadem, and on the other side a harp crowned, with the king's title, JACOBVS DEI GRATIA MAGNÆ BRITANNIÆ FRANCIÆ ET HIBERNIÆ REX; with a privy-mark to be set upon them, from time to time, whereby to discern and distinguish them, and to be altered according to occasion, for preventing the falsifying and counterfeiting of the same". It was also stipulated that the tokens should weigh not less than 6 gr. (i.e. 1 lb. avoirdupois of copper would yield 24*s.* 3*d.* in farthings) and that after the next feast of St. John Baptist, the leaden tokens should no longer be made or used.'

In the first paragraph of the above quotation an estimate is made of the profit to the king that the striking of such tokens under patent would yield. As a further sidelight on the money to be made by making money, and bearing in mind that all present English coins are no more than tokens, the quotation is continued.

'The new farthings were to be distributed by Lord Harington at the rate of 21*s*. in farthings for 20*s*. sterling and, for a period of one year, a special concession was granted whereby anyone in possession of more tokens than he could conveniently use might rechange them into sterling at the same rate. By the original terms of the patent Lord Harington was to receive half the profit from the issue of the tokens, but it appears that before the contract was actually sealed the king changed his mind on learning that the grant was worth £60,000, and finally fixed Lord Harington's share at £25,000, ordering that the surplus should be paid to himself.'

Through succession and acquisition, the patent passed through various hands, until the reign of Charles I.

'From all accounts,' says Mr. Wilson Peck, 'the tokens were extremely unpopular from the start. Directions were issued to all mayors, sheriffs, justices of the peace, bailiffs, constables, and headboroughs to do all that lay in their power to assist in

Plate 21 DOMINION COINAGE: SOUTH AFRICA, INDIA

88. The Pound piece of the Union of South Africa. In its move towards an entirely independent status, the Dominion of South Africa has dropped the name 'Sovereign', and resumed the correct title for this gold piece of the One Pound.
89. Silver Shilling of the Dominion of South Africa. Coins in gold and silver are still struck (1966).
90. Silver Rupee of William IV (1830–37). Issued by the British East India Company before India became an Empire of the British Crown.

ELIZABETH II REGINA
SUID AFRIKA · 1953 · SOUTH AFRICA
88
ELIZABETH II REGINA
SOUTH AFRICA · 1953 · SUID-AFRIKA
89
WILLIAM IIII, KING.
EAST INDIA COMPANY
ONE
RUPEE
1835
90

91
ONE DOLLAR
1895
壹
圓
92
1758
QUOCUNQUE JECERIS STABIT
93
C. BROOKE RAJAH
SARAWAK
TWENTY 1915 CENTS
20

promoting their circulation. Nevertheless, several counties, notably Derbyshire, Staffordshire, Flintshire, and Denbighshire refused to take them, and those counties that did accept them took such small quantities that the total value of the farthings distributed during the first six months amounted to barely £600. Rechange was also very heavy at first owing to the spread of a rumour that the tokens were to be altered and that the old ones would then be unacceptable.'

By the beginning of the reign of Charles I it was obvious that the attempts of the Government to dabble in the issuing of tokens was far from successful. Large quantities of forgeries had appeared, workmen were not infrequently forced to take their entire wages in farthings, and the situation had got out of control. The matter was considered on various occasions by the Court of Star Chamber, and after a great deal of consideration by committees, the sheriff and council of the City of London, and other bodies, the issues of this series of tokens ceased, probably in December, 1644. All this manœuvring is given in considerable detail in the catalogue referred to above.

During the Commonwealth further patterns for a copper

Plate 22 COLONIAL AND ISLAND COINS: BRITISH DOLLAR, ISLE OF MAN, SARAWAK

91. The handsome silver Dollar, struck for circulation in the Far East.
92. Penny, struck in bronze, of the Isle of Man when the island was the possession of the Dukes of Atholl. A parallel can be drawn between this and the next illustration.
93. Silver Twenty-Cent piece of the colony of Sarawak. The Rajah of Sarawak, Charles Brooke, and his successors, issued their own coins. The romantic story of Sarawak is a typical page in English colonial history.

token coinage were prepared, but a regular issue failed to materialise. This led to a reappearance of tokens issued by private traders and later by towns. They appeared in small numbers at first, but the issue greatly increased between 1660 and 1669, and their circulation continued until 1674.

These private issues form a second stage in the token coinage issue of the country. As has been described, the first reasonably clear-cut stage in token issues was that of the royal patent issues. The second, that of the private issues, is even more clear-cut, and is usually regarded by numismatists as an entirely separate series, referred to as the 'seventeenth-century trader's tokens series'.

In the event these tokens have found a place in the cabinet of many collectors, partly because of their local interest, but mainly because they attained during the period an almost official status. They met a genuine need which the authorities did little to relieve.

For those interested in local history as well as to many coin collectors these tokens are of considerable importance. Normally they contained the name of the issuer, and sometimes that of his wife or business partner, and a small representation of the arms of his guild or his recognised trading sign. The seventeenth century was the golden age of shop and trading signs which, in the towns and villages, hung in profusion before the business premises. Many of the public could not read, and these signs, as well as indicating the trade followed by the various shopkeepers, acted as an advertisement. Many of the devices used were very elaborate and wrought with considerable skill, often in bright colours. Most of them have long since disappeared, but the better class of modern inn sign gives some idea of what they were like. Here lay the beginnings of our present advertising technique, our electric skysigns and illuminated advertisements.

A considerable number of the trade and guild signs used have survived on the seventeenth-century tokens, and the series as a whole has received considerable attention and has been well written up. In many places much local history has been brought to light by a study of the tokens which survive, supplemented by parish records.

By 1672, when a copper coinage was at last ready for circulation, the issue of tokens was suppressed, though records show that it did not die away completely for some two years after that date.

But if the seventeenth-century tokens are often accepted by serious collectors as almost official, the same cannot be said of the series which appeared in the eighteenth century.

These commenced about 1784, and were resultant upon the fact that during the reign of George III, until the re-equipment of the Royal Mint and the new coinage of 1816–17, both copper and silver went almost entirely out of circulation. Another factor, already referred to, has a bearing on the issue of these tokens. This was the advance made in coining by Messrs. Boulton and Watt. The wars with France (1793–1815) and the American war (1812–15) also had a considerable bearing on the disappearance of silver and copper from circulation and the absence of new issues in these metals.

One of the main objections to a copper currency had, from its inception, been the relative ease with which it was counterfeited. For example, in 1789 Boulton, who was in process of urging a well-manufactured copper coinage upon the Government – a coinage which, if produced by his improved methods, would not be easily forged – observed: 'In the course of my journeys I observe that I receive upon an average two-thirds counterfeit halfpence for change at tollgates &c., and I believe the evil is daily increasing as the spurious money is carried into circulation by the lowest class of manufacturers who pay with it the principal part of the wages of the poor people they employ.'

Finally, a further circumstance was the friendship which existed between Boulton and John Wilkinson, the iron-master.

As a result of all these contributory factors a series of tokens appeared, mostly pennies, halfpennies and farthings. They were mainly coined at Boulton's factory, and began with the Anglesey pennies and halfpennies of the Parys Mines Company.

From the collector's point of view they have yet to attain the same status as the issues of the preceding century; but they are still not without interest, and the series has its rare pieces. Their comparative lack of interest to the collector is partly due to the fact that, instead of being highly individual pieces, many of them were issued by local authorities and large trading firms. The day of the individual was already passing with the onset of the industrial revolution. Clearing-houses were established in various large towns for dealing with the tokens, London, Liverpool and Manchester being among the chief. Most of the tokens bore on their edges the names of the towns at which they could be redeemed.

One point of interest these tokens have. Though many of them depict various allegorical devices or municipal arms, a large number feature local buildings, many of which have long since been altered or entirely swept away. London is perhaps pre-eminent in this respect, a large series of finely executed pennies showing various famous buildings, but apart from such local interest the eighteenth century tokens have little to offer. Their issue was suspended in 1797 when Boulton received a contract for regal copper coinage. At least his well-executed tokens had proved how accurately copper could be coined.

Once more tokens were to appear – in the nineteenth century. This time the issue took various forms. Many tokens were struck by municipalities, Birmingham being a typical example. Local firms and manufacturers also issued tokens, which in some cases were original strikings and in others took the form of foreign coins, generally the long-suffering eight reales of Spain, which were over-stamped with the firm's name or device. These were paid out to employees who, in many cases, could only redeem them at some local firm stipulated by the issuer, in return for provisions of food and the like.

Most of the original strikings were in copper, but alongside them there exists a series of silver tokens, issued about the same time, the commonest denominations being shillings and sixpences though half-crowns and crowns do exist. Again they were mainly issued by municipalities and large trading firms. There were also the Bank of England dollars, to which reference has already been made and which are in fact a form of token, called into existence by the scarcity of regal issues. There were also a very few gold tokens.

In the main, the nineteenth-century series of tokens commands even less interest than the eighteenth-century series among serious collectors, save that the countermarked pieces referred to above are of some importance, in that they were issued by firms, some of whose successors are trading today. They contain a lot of 'family history' and so appeal to a certain type of collector, if only because many of them are crown-size pieces. The Cockayne, Lingford and Whetmore sale catalogues contain large numbers of these pieces, and from these catalogues something of their interest can be gleaned.

The issue of tokens has not quite died away even today, though they have mainly been superseded by paper tickets and coupons. Various tokens, mainly uniface examples, still appear occasionally, issued as rebates on sale prices by retailers.

During the second half of the nineteenth and the early years of the twentieth centuries, when municipalities began to take an interest in the establishment of local transport facilities, tokens were frequently issued in various materials for uses similar to those now performed by the paper ticket. Included in this series are encased postage stamps, issued for use on the Paris tramways, 'plastic' tokens, issued for London, Birmingham and other tramways (p. 87), metal tokens, issued for Liverpool buses and trams, and metal ferry tokens. As yet these latter issues do not command much interest among collectors. In this series also figure Directors' passes and tickets, which most of the railways issued during their formative period and which, at least till nationalisation, still survived in the case of a few of the more highly-placed railway officials. Finally there are tokens issued to hop-pickers, and a series known as Scottish Communion Tokens, of ecclesiastical origin.

The Fitzwilliam Museum, Cambridge, has some fine examples of leaden 'Bishop's Tokens', used by choirboys in an interesting and ancient custom. The quaint story that lies behind them is told by Mr. J. B. Caldecott, and recorded in the *Transactions of the International Numismatic Congress*, held in London in 1936. From this account of a now forgotten ceremony we quote the following.*

'On St. Nicholas Day (December 6), that of the patron saint of children, one of the choristers of cathedrals, abbeys, and many larger churches was elected as a boy bishop, by the votes of

* At least a part of this ceremony was recently revived.

the other choristers and held office until Innocents' Day or Childermas (December 28) and during that period exercised the functions of the real prelate or abbot.

'He is known . . . in English, as St. Nicholas Bishop and Barne Bishop, the latter from the old word bairn for child.

'He was attended by other choristers as dean and prebendaries, celebrated Mass, and preached a sermon on Innocents' Day, two of which, evidently written by an older hand, are extant, one preached at St. Paul's (fifteenth century) and the other at Gloucester, 1588.

'It might be interesting to speculate what the real bishop did during the period of his juvenile copy; he probably retired to one of his numerous country manors for a well-earned holiday.

'The boy bishop made a circuit of the town blessing the people and collecting money from house to house, and during his term of office made a progress to the larger houses of his district.

'There seems to be a general impression that the boy bishop's reign of office was a burlesque of the services of the church; but that, in England at any rate, he and his attendants conducted themselves in a proper manner is shown by the statutes of St. Paul's School in which Dean Colet directs that the scholars "shall every Childermas – that is Innocents' Day – come to Paule's Church and hear the Childe Byshop's sermon and after be at high Masse and each of them offer a penny to the Childe bishop and with them the maisters and surveyers of the schole".

'The leaden pieces which are the subject of this paper have been found only in Bury St. Edmunds, so one can safely assume that their issue in England was confined to the abbey there, one that had a long tradition of coinage rights.'

The actual pieces themselves, being struck in lead, have only survived in small numbers. As stated above, the Fitzwilliam Museum has some very fine specimens in its collection. Caldecott divides the known issues into three categories: (1) Large size, struck in imitation of groats; (2) Large size, crude fabric; and (3) Small size, struck in imitation of pennies. Of these the first series is the finest, showing on the obverse the mitred head of a bishop, while the reverse bears every resemblance to the original groat. The later series show a general degeneration of workmanship. Concluding his paper Mr. Caldecott says, 'It may be of interest to record that the boy bishop has been revived in some churches, notably at Salisbury Cathedral, during the last year or two, and that this cathedral possesses a tomb of a boy in bishop's vestments which has been considered to be that of a boy bishop who died during his period of office.'

Thus again we see one of those numismatic side-lines of interest. There are many such with interesting stories behind them.

CHAPTER NINE

Empire and Commonwealth Coins

NO GENERAL work on numismatics having special reference to the coinage of England would be complete without some reference to the coinages of the Dominions, Colonies and Protectorates. These territories, once known as the British Empire, are, in these days of broader views, the British Commonwealth of Nations. Their various coinages are commanding increasing interest among collectors. This is partly stimulated by the appearance of new reference works, after an interval of some sixty years, including one in the series of books to which this volume belongs.* Interest is also stimulated by the constant development of the territories themselves and of the whole body of the Commonwealth. This development affects the coinage, if only to change the titles in its legends, and new series and denominations appear. In some instances, an increasing number, the coinage is placed on a decimal basis after many years on the binary system.

As far back as 1600 the Government of Elizabeth I issued a series of coins for use in trading ventures to the Indies. These denominations were four in number, and consisted of a crown-size piece in silver, the Eight Testernes, with subdivisions. The coins became known as the 'Portcullis money' on account of the main feature of the reverse design, the crowned portcullis of the Tudors. The larger piece also came to be known as the eight reales or ryals. Recent research, however, has established documentary proof of the correct title for this series.

These interesting pieces are now rare, and the larger is often included by collectors of English crowns among their pieces. They were issued to compete with the Spanish eight reales. This coin was in use among the traders of the world, as stated elsewhere, and had achieved near-universal acceptance. In the face of such established custom the series failed to find acceptance, and the issue was terminated. By many it is looked

* *British Commonwealth Coinage.*

upon as the first colonial coinage. A not very appropriate title; but they were the first venture in striking coins for use overseas at the beginning of that period of national development when the first colonisation efforts began to lead to the establishment of the present British Commonwealth of Nations. Even so the coins were not intended for use in those lands to the west, where explorers were beginning to open up trade and settlement in the teeth of Spanish opposition. It is an interesting speculation if, had these coins been acceptable for the purpose for which they were intended, they might also have come into use in trade with the Americas, and so have been an early influence on later American coinages, as was the eight reales.

The next phase was the coinage issued, by authority from the Crown in many cases, by the great trading companies and in particular the East India Company. This company continued such issues until it was 'nationalised' in 1858, when the Government of India was assumed by the Crown. The East India Company's issues as a whole were very complex. In India they were struck at several mints, and for other countries, such as Sumatra or Malacca, where the company traded, coins were often struck in England, particularly by Boulton and Watt at Soho, Birmingham. The company's series as a whole present a considerable amount of numismatic interest and not a few problems. So far as India was concerned the company's coinage was followed by a monetary system based on the rupee, a system which stemmed from beginnings under William IV.

As the Empire grew and developed, speaking in the broadest terms, the coinage development followed a fairly uniform plan. The series of any possession frequently started with a makeshift coinage. This often consisted of miscellaneous coins, sometimes cut into sections and/or countermarked. Local issues might be put into circulation, either struck in England or made on the spot. The West Indies, the early American settlements, Canada, South Africa and Australia give us examples of this. In the first our old friend the Spanish and Spanish-American eight reales once more came into use. It was countermarked, cut into sections, pierced and generally maltreated to serve as local currency. In Canada and Australia local tokens were put into circulation: in the American colonies a series of rough coins was struck on the spot, and supplemented by coins struck at home and exported. Perhaps the most common stage of development was the putting into circulation of English coins as struck for home use. In some West Indian islands this still holds, and only in 1940 did New Zealand start to issue its own pennies and halfpennies.

In the larger territories the next stage would be the establishment of a branch of the Royal Mint, usually under the direction of a mint master sent out from London. This establishment would strike either coins on the English pattern or local issues. In South Africa the mint at Pretoria, originally founded under lease, *circa* 1891, by the National Bank of the South African Republic as the State Mint of the Transvaal, became a branch of the Royal Mint from 1922 until 1941. It then became the South African Mint and no longer a branch of the Royal Mint. In Australia branch mints were established at Melbourne, Sydney and Perth.

The final phase, as in South Africa and Canada, is the taking over by the local government of the branch mint, which then usually strikes coins of a suitable local design, if it has not already begun to do so. When Australia changed to decimal currency in February 1966 a new mint, The Royal Australian Mint, was built and opened at Canberra.

In the smaller territories coins would be supplied from the Royal Mint in London, or through their subcontractors, to local requirements. Changes are gradual, but in main outline this pattern is often followed, As an example, Hong Kong in 1960 decided to issue dollar coins. These were issued from London, but were in fact struck by the successors of Boulton and Watt, Heaton and Co., now The Mint, Birmingham, Limited, and by the successors of the Kings Norton Metal Company, now Imperial Chemical Industries, Metals Division. In both cases the old Mint marks, 'H' and 'KN', were retained. There was once a branch mint in Hong Kong, but it failed financially and was closed down after 1868. Since then the coins for the Colony have been struck officially in London, but mainly at the subcontractors' mints.

In some countries where a coinage was already in circulation, such as a territory taken over from another power, this existing coinage has, in some cases, been perpetuated for a time. Ultimately a local coinage would be put into circulation, this again being officially a Royal Mint issue, but often struck by subcontractors and bearing their mint mark. All this leads to increased interest, and also problems, from the collector's point of view.

Sufficient has been said to indicate that even a brief look at some of the coinages circulating in the British Commonwealth of Nations will reveal many points of interest.

In Canada the monetary system follows on the lines of that of the United States, being on the decimal system with the silver dollar as the unit. This particular piece, now only struck in small numbers, has been largely replaced by bank-notes, but the half-dollar and the smaller denominations are still in day-to-day use. A complete set of the Canadian denominations from the dollar to the cent was struck in 1953, partly to mark the coronation of Elizabeth II. The custom so established has been continued annually, to the satisfaction of collectors.

In the early days of Canadian history, during the French régime, the coins issued followed the French monetary system as then in use. They are rare pieces now, and of particular interest in that the French monetary system had not then been placed on a decimal basis. Following the British conquest of Canada, the coins and tokens issued were at first of the British binary system, but with the growth of the United States this system became untenable. In the days of the American colonies such coinage as was issued was in locally struck shillings and subdivisions, but once the rising power of the United States was made manifest it was obvious that its neighbour, Canada, must fall into line. This it did, after a period of token coinage, *circa* 1858. So grew up the decimal system in use in Canada today, and from these developments has grown a coinage series of great interest – one receiving increasing attention from collectors and historians. Those who have faith in the future of the nation of Canada, and a certain amount of inside knowledge concerning its natural resources, might be prepared to forecast that the day may well come when the Canadian nation will wield more power than does the United States of America. What interesting changes this will bring about in the north

American coinages may be revealed in the twenty-first or twenty-second centuries. By that time the parent country, Great Britain, will probably long since have been forced, by simple 'starvation' tactics, on to a decimal basis for its coinage. From such speculations it can be perceived how live, changing and interesting is the whole subject of numismatics.

To return to the past and the present: Australia, like New Zealand, had, till 1966, the same denominations of coinage as has Great Britain, but no half-crown has so far been issued in Australia. This is of interest in that the basic silver unit of that country is, as in Great Britain, the crown piece, a coin which has been issued in Australia from time to time. The first crown struck was to mark the coronation of George VI (1937), and a second crown was struck in 1938. Since then no crown has appeared, not even to mark the coronation of the present Queen. Since Australia has now placed its coinage on a decimal basis it may well be that no further crown, as such, will ever appear. The new fifty-cent piece is only of half-crown size.

In New Zealand the first crown was struck (in London) to mark the Jubilee of George V, 1935. Since the reverse design commemorated the signing of the Treaty of Waitangi, 1840, the piece had become known as the 'Waitangi Crown'. The real centenary of the Treaty was commemorated in the coinage by a special half-crown, struck in 1940.

A second New Zealand crown piece was struck in 1949, in preparation for the proposed Royal Tour of Australasia in that year. Owing to failing health, George VI was unable to undertake this tour. Many of the crowns were therefore melted down, but through vigorous action on the part of numismatists enough were saved from the melting-pot to be available to collectors.

A third New Zealand crown was struck in 1953, to mark the coronation of Elizabeth II, and it, as all other New Zealand coinage since its inception in 1933, was struck at the Royal Mint in London, from which mint the New Zealand issues have continued.

Since New Zealand too is on the verge of a decimal coinage system, this may also be the last crown, as such, to appear. When these two economically powerful members of the British Commonwealth have decimalised their coinage, the 'starvation' tactics against the British binary system will operate with increased force, particularly as the next country to be considered, South Africa, has already placed its coinage on the decimal system.

In South Africa, until February 1961, the same denominations were in use as those of Great Britain. The coins had local designs and bilingual legends. This heavily gold-bearing country was the only one to strike a gold pound and half-pound in the new coinage series following the coronation of Elizabeth II in 1953. Here it should be mentioned that, while the first South African coinage, issued in 1923, included the sovereign and half-sovereign, only the Royal Mint or a branch thereof can issue sovereigns. As mentioned above, this branch of the Royal Mint became the South African Mint in 1941. Having thus severed all connections with the Royal Mint, sovereigns could no longer be issued. The denominations were therefore designated the pound and half-pound.

In past time, in the pre-British era in South Africa, many and various coins from devious countries served as money in South Africa, culminating in a series of coins bearing the head of President Kruger. This series was struck for him in Germany, leading to a well-known numismatic mistake, the so-called double-shaft sovereign. After the South African War this issue of coins naturally ceased, though the pieces were accepted in circulation for some years. They still evoke considerable interest among local collectors.

After much legislation and debate a local coinage, as stated above, was struck in 1923, to be followed in 1961 by a decimal local coinage. On this the head of the Sovereign of the British Commonwealth no longer appeared. Its place was taken by the head of Van Riebeeck and the silver unit, the crown, is now displaced by a fifty-cent piece. The pound and half-pound have become the two- and one-rand pieces.

In the rest of Africa the coinages of the British Commonwealth territories have been many and various. In the east, Kenya, Uganda, Tanganyika, and Mombasa eventually arrived at a common coinage, struck at the Royal Mint and at various other mints both at home and in the Commonwealth. In this collection of territories, Mombasa was the first with its own coinage, the remainder following as the country was opened up.

Southern Rhodesia started a coinage of its own in 1932, and the later Federation of Northern and Southern Rhodesia and Nyasaland had a coinage common to the three countries. The original Southern Rhodesian coinage ceased to be issued.

To the west the Gold Coast early had its own coinage, in 1796, while Sierra Leone was five years earlier, its first dollar appearing in 1791. The Gold Coast issued an entirely new coinage as soon as it became the independent state of Ghana, and Nigeria, on attaining independent status, also issued coins of its own design, but retaining the head of the Queen. Both these coinages were struck at the Royal Mint.

In the African countries as a whole the decimal and binary systems are in use according to the territories concerned. The Rhodesias have always used the latter system while the East African countries have an apparently curious mixture of florins, shillings and various denominations of cents. In the west the binary system has been continued. Recent changes in the government and status of the one-time African colonial territories have brought many new coinages into being within the last few years. Until the companion volume *British Commonwealth Coinage* is revised their details will have to be ascertained elsewhere.

Even tiny St. Helena once had a small coinage of its own, while the Seychelles Islands group commenced their own coinage as recently as 1939. This coinage is on the rupee basis, fitting with that in use in India, until that country turned to the decimal system in 1957. The Republic of Pakistan continued with the rupee system.

The coinages of Gibraltar, Malta and Cyprus have been through many changes, some of them quite recent, and the coinage once issued under British rule for Palestine has now passed into the realm of the collector. In Aden, as in many Eastern countries not under British rule, the British sovereign, and forgeries of it, are still in use.

Ceylon has a long coinage history while under British rule, and farther away in Malaya and the Straits Settlements a prolific coinage, based on the British dollar, once a handsome silver piece, was put into circulation in 1871. The coinage of Sarawak has an interesting history of its own, while British North Borneo, New Guinea, Fiji – even Java – have or have had coinages emanating from British rule or Commonwealth status.

On the other side of the world the early coinages of the West Indian group of islands, already referred to, are of considerable interest. The problems of attributing the many locally issued cut and countermarked pieces to the large number of islands are formidable, and continue to interest numismatists. On the mainland, British Guiana and British Honduras long had coinages of their own. Nearer home the Channel Islands, the Isle of Man, even little Lundy – all have numismatic histories.

It has thus been demonstrated that considerable interest is to be derived from the study of British Commonwealth Coinage and more detailed work on the subject will be found elsewhere.* For those who want a wider horizon than the long history which the British coinage has to offer, there is here a considerable panorama worthy of study.

In connection with the coinages of the British Commonwealth of nations it must be remembered that many of the countries which form or have formed its constituent parts have long histories of their own. Many of them were civilised and fully populated long before the era of British rule. It follows that the coins issued during that period are often only a short phase in a very long numismatic story. Many of the countries have been independent of outside rule, others have belonged to different nations. Some have parted from direct British rule and achieved independent administration. Others have been ceded to foreign nations, while still others have severed all connection with the British Empire or Commonwealth. In such cases the numismatic history passes into and out of the British Empire and Commonwealth phase and goes its own way. India and Pakistan are excellent examples of the first category, South Africa of the last.

Throughout recorded history as empires rise and fall and as boundary lines change, so the numismatic story of the various countries of the world continues to develop, offering a

* *British Commonwealth Coinage.*

never-ending source of study to the archæologist, the historian, the economist, the geographer, and the numismatist alike. No one book can make any attempt to deal with the world picture of a subject that touches at some point almost every other form of academic research. The same opportunities for study and the same sources of interest exist in regard to every country, and in whichever country an individual may take an interest, there exists a numismatic history worthy of his attention.

Plate 23 COMMONWEALTH COINS

94. Bronze Penny of Jersey, commemorating the liberation from German occupation. Some numismatic confusion has been caused by the use of the same revenue die for some Pennies of Elizabeth II. In any case the piece was not issued in 1945 and actually counts as undated. The date 1945 only commemorates the liberation, the coin illustrated being struck in 1949.
95. Bronze Eight Doubles of Guernsey.
96. Nickel Penny of British West Africa. In this territory, as in East Africa, New Guinea and Fiji, a number of minor coins without portrait but with the title of Edward VIII are in circulation.
97. Lundy Island, privately owned, had, for a short time, a token currency of Puffins and Half-Puffins. Their circulation was later suspended (Bronze).
98. Silver Nine Piastres of Cyprus.
99. The Rock also had its own currency for a time. Illustrated is the Two Quarts bronze piece.
100. One of the few non-circular modern coins, the nickel One Piastre of Cyprus. A few Commonwealth countries have or have had square coins, the Straits Settlements being an example.

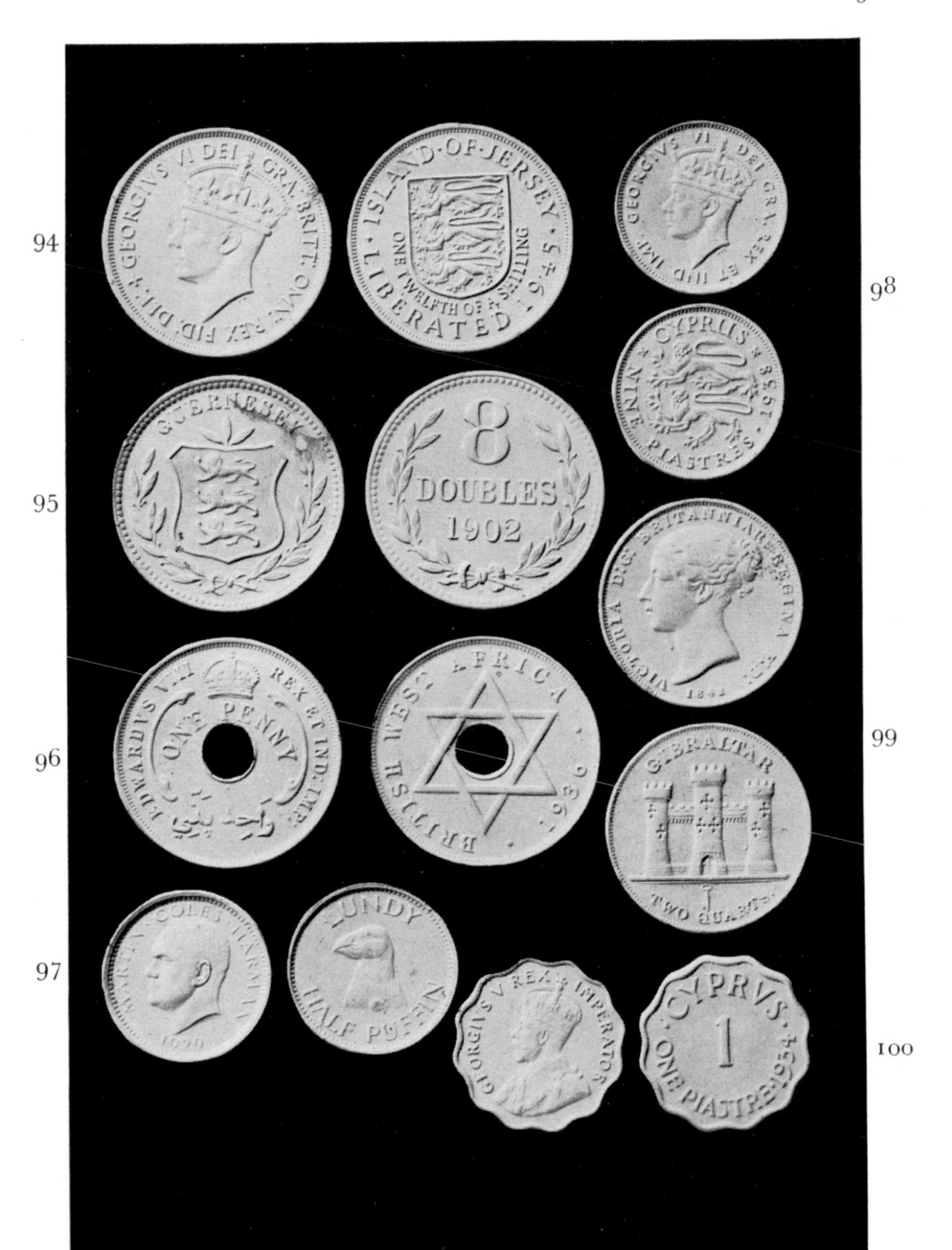
94
95
96
97
98
99
100
GEORGIVS VI DEI GRA: BRITT: OMN: REX FID: DEF:
ISLAND OF JERSEY
LIBERATED 1945
ONE TWELFTH OF A SHILLING
GUERNESEY
8
DOUBLES
1902
EDWARDVS VIII REX ET IND: IMP:
ONE PENNY
BRITISH WEST AFRICA
1936
GEORGIVS VI DEI GRA: REX ET IND: IMP:
CYPRUS
PIASTRES
1938
VICTORIA D: G: BRITANNIAR: REGINA
GIBRALTAR
TWO QUARTS
LUNDY
HALF PUFFIN
GEORGIVS V REX ET IMPERATOR
CYPRVS
1
ONE PIASTRE 1934

Plate 24

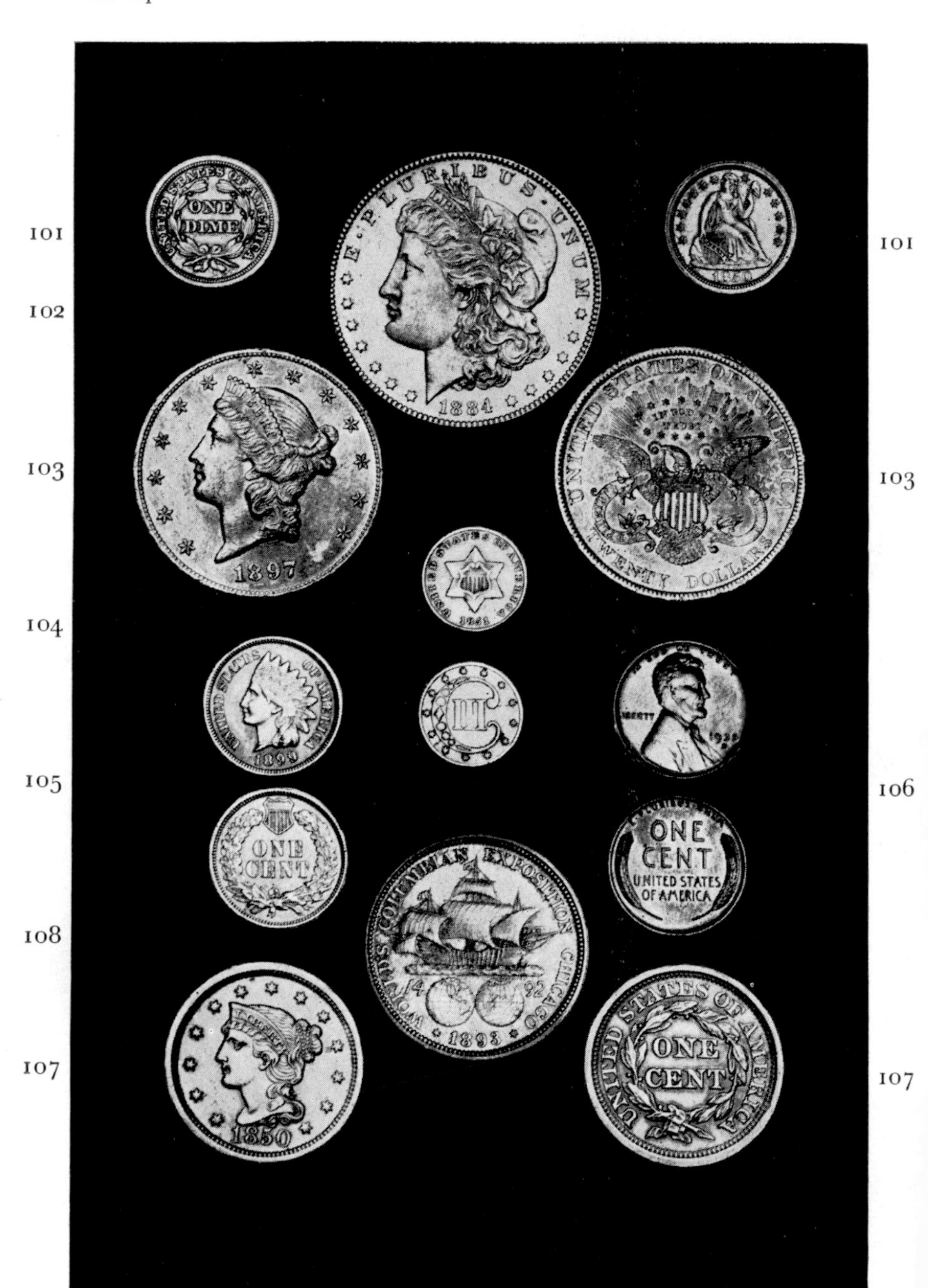
101
101
102
E · PLURIBUS · UNUM
1884
ONE DIME
103
103
1897
UNITED STATES OF AMERICA
TWENTY DOLLARS
104
105
106
ONE CENT
ONE CENT
UNITED STATES
OF AMERICA
108
WORLD'S COLUMBIAN EXPOSITION CHICAGO
14 92
1893
107
107
1850
UNITED STATES OF AMERICA
ONE CENT

CHAPTER TEN

The American collector and what he collects

BY REASON of his environment and the fact that his nation has come into being in a comparatively short space of historic time, the American collector, in the majority of cases, tends to collect on a somewhat different plan from that of his European counterpart. Speaking broadly, and throughout these pages we have always tried to speak thus, American collectors fall into two main categories. The first collects the coins from the old world from which he or his ancestors came. The second collects the coins of the country to which he belongs. It is not quite as simple as that, since so many threads run through the pattern of any form of collecting. To divide the interests of almost any numismatist into a series of watertight compartments is an exercise doomed to failure but, taking the broad view, these two main categories bear some semblance of truth.

Into the former category the American collector has thrown

Plate 24 UNITED STATES COINS

101. Reverse and obverse of the "Liberty seated" type dime, (Silver).
102. Obverse of silver dollar. No longer struck, but still in circulation, mainly in Western states.
103. Gold twenty dollar piece.
104. Silver three cent piece.
105. The bronze Indian head cent.
106. Bronze Lincoln head cent.
107. Copper large cent.
108. One of the many silver commemorative half dollars. This example, the reverse only being shown, commemorated the fourth centenary of the discovery of America. A head representing Columbus appeared on the obverse, and the coin was sold at the World's Columbian Exposition in Chicago in 1893.

These pieces are only representative. Many designs for the various denominations have appeared.

all that energy for which he is famous. He has studied and researched into the numismatic histories of the old world with a regard worthy of the subject of his studies. Some of the finest collections of the multitudinous coinages of the old world exist and have existed and continue to be built up in the cabinets and museums of America. Little more need be said of the American collector in this first category. He is at one with his contemporaries in the old world. He appreciates its numismatic history, its art and culture, and its various civilisations.

In the second category, the most numerous, we come across a form of collecting less common in the old world, an intense preoccupation with a short-historied home coinage. Faced with a very wide historical field, the European collector does not as a rule specialise so much in what he considers modern issues. He may start his collecting life with such series, but as the wide scope offered begins to be appreciated, the historic period of the European's collection tends to grow. Finally the collection may specialise in a series which, to an American, may appear quite remote. Without stepping aside from the coinage of his own country such a possibility is not open to the American collector. He is therefore driven to minute specialisation if he is to concentrate on the numismatic material that his country has to offer.

This form of collecting can perhaps be epitomised by saying that a collector will purchase many hundreds of minor denominations, often fresh from the American mints, and study them for slight die varieties or errors with an intensity worthy of a larger subject. So far is this carried that at least one American numismatic organisation publishes periodic lists, bearing a strong resemblance to the stocks and shares lists in *The Times*, showing which variety of minor denomination has risen in value and which has fallen.

Having gone far towards the exhaustion of the coinage of the United States in this intensity the American collector has turned to the coinage of Canada, and is turning to the modern issues of the British Commonwealth of Nations and to those of Europe as a whole. Various catalogues provide epitomised information on all these fields of modern coinage.

There is nothing new in this form of collecting. It has been done, and is still being done, with the minor issues of modern

British and European coins by European collectors, but not on the scale attained in America, though in recent years the rapid growth of collectors in Britain has greatly increased this form of collecting.

In the United States series of coins, what is there to collect? The field is made as wide as possible and starts with the coins and tokens of the British American colonies. Under this heading some catalogues take in Bermuda – the Somers Islands as they were sometimes called – though strictly this small and rare series of coins belongs to the British Commonwealth series. There is a numismatic bridge here, in that Sir George Somers, who was wrecked on the islands in 1609, was on his way to the Virginia Plantation.

Of the colonial pieces proper the first appear to be the shillings, sixpences and threepences struck in Massachusetts (New England). Before they appeared shells, known as wampum, corn, pelts and bullets were frequently offered in lieu of coins.

From this custom has stemmed a form of collecting of great interest in America, that of curious currency. This consists of any object not a coin which took the place, or might possibly have taken the place, of the non-existent coinage. Such collecting needs as much care as the collecting of Greek and Roman coins, with all their problems of forgeries and later counterfeits. It is too easy to convince the gullible that some odd object might have passed as money in Colonial days.

The New England coins were struck as the result of agitation which reached its peak in 1651. At that time the Civil Wars in England caused the agitation to be ignored, with the natural result that the colonists took matters into their own hands in 1652. The pieces struck under a General Court order of 1652 were the pieces mentioned above. They were struck from West Indian bullion, at an improvised mint just outside Boston. They consisted of plain, roughly circular flans, with the letters NE on the obverse and the value in Roman figures on the reverse. They were the first of the short series of American hammered coinage.

Since they were easy to forge they were quickly followed by a series for which much more complicated dies had been prepared. These pieces have an outer legend, and a tree – willow, oak or pine – as the device in the field. On the reverse appeared the date and value. The coins were dated 1652, with the exception of the Oak Tree twopence, which was authorised in 1662 and is so dated. This series of 'tree' coins was actually issued for some thirty years, but bore the date of 1652 because Charles II disapproved of the issue. Provided the date was always the same it would be difficult to prove that the colonists were continuing to issue the coins after the date which appeared on them. This series was abandoned in 1682. There are many die varieties and numerous forgeries, mainly contemporary. Several authoritative works have been published on the series, and collecting should not be undertaken without one of these works on hand.

In Maryland the second Lord Baltimore began a coinage in 1658, struck in England, which consisted of shillings, sixpences and fourpences in silver and a small copper penny. Naturally these are of much more sophisticated workmanship, and are all now very rare pieces. They show the head of Lord Baltimore on the obverse, with the family arms on the reverse, save on the penny, which has a ducal coronet.

In November, 1681, Mark Newby arrived in America from Dublin and brought with him some copper halfpence which are believed to have been struck in that city in 1678. They received wide circulation in the New Jersey Province, being sanctioned by the General Assembly in May, 1682. They show on the obverse a kneeling king playing a harp, and on the reverse St. Patrick surrounded by people. There is also a similar farthing, on the reverse of which the saint is shown driving away reptiles.

An Englishman named William Wood obtained a patent from George I to make copper tokens for Ireland and the American Colonies. Though the first pieces which were struck were undated the later are dated 1722, 1723, 1724 and 1733. They show the head of George I on the obverse and a rose on the reverse. A number of coins intended for Ireland and struck by Wood, consisting of halfpennies and farthings dated 1722, 1723 and 1724, were also sent to America for use, as they proved unpopular in Ireland. A number of French colonies in America also had coins, mainly sous, dated down to 1767.

These miscellaneous early series were followed by coins issued by the various states, New Hampshire, New York, Vermont, Connecticut, Massachusetts and New Jersey, offering many interesting and sometimes rare pieces of this period.

Preceding the first United States issues are many early pieces, patterns, proofs, private issues, tokens, dollars thought to have been struck in Birmingham, Anglo-American tokens, Washington tokens, Pitt tokens, and the like. This interesting series also contains many rarities, much sought after by the American collector.

In dealing with these early American issues – a series very important to the American collector – we have gone into little or no detail. That is the province of the American writer, who has produced many working catalogues of the whole series of American coins.

At this point we come to the great divide, when the United States were established, and when Canada began to issue its own tokens and coins. In the latter series there are established annual catalogues. These very detailed works keep collectors of the Canadian series of coins in close touch with the values of the various coins and tokens. In the United States are similar annual catalogues and statements of values, and from *A Guide Book of United States Coins*, by R. S. Yeoman, we quote the history of the first coins to be issued by the then newly constituted United States of America.

'The first coins issued by authority of the United States,' says Mr. Yeoman, 'were the "Fugio" cents. Entries in the Journal of Congress supply interesting information about proceedings relating to this coinage.

'"Saturday, April 21, 1787. . . . That the board of treasury be authorised to contract for three hundred tons of copper coin of the federal standard, agreeable to the proposition of Mr. James Jarvis. . . . That it be coined at the expense of the contractors, etc."

'On Friday, July 6, 1786, there was "Resolved, that the board of treasury direct the contractor for the copper coinage to stamp on one side of each piece the following, viz.: thirteen circles linked together, a small circle in the middle, with the words 'United States' round it; in the centre, the words 'We are one'; on the other side of the same piece the following device, viz.: a dial with the hours expressed on the face of it; a meridian sun above on one side of which is the word 'Fugio', and on the other the year in figures '1787'; below the dial the words 'Mind Your Business.'"

'The legends have been credited to Benjamin Franklin by many, and the coin, as a consequence, has been referred to as the Franklin Cent. These cents were coined in New Haven, Conn., and (it has been suggested) also in New York City, Rupert, Vt., and elsewhere. The dies were made by Abel Buel of New Haven.'

Thus we see the birth of a coinage which was to be a great power in years to come, a power to which much of the world was to defer in less than two hundred years.

Of these Fugio Cents there are a number of varieties, some of them so rare that values cannot be quoted for them by the cataloguer.

From them we pass on to the first United States Mint issues, and again quote from Yeoman's catalogue.

'Various devices were proposed for our coins just preceding the establishment of the mint.

'Hamilton, in January 1791, in his long report to the House on questions of finance, said, "The devices of the coins ought to be emblematical but without losing sight of simplicity." Many members of the House favoured a representation of the president's head on the obverse of each coin. Others considered the idea a monarchial practice. Washington is believed to have expressed disapproval of the use of his portrait on our coins. The majority considered a figure emblematic of Liberty more appropriate and the Senate finally concurred in this opinion.

'Thomas Birch was an engraver employed at designing proposed devices for our coins. He engraved the dies for the disme and half-disme. He has also been associated with a large copper cent of unusual design, which is known as the Birch Cent. Henry Voigt, first chief-coiner of the mint, prepared a similar, small-sized copper cent.'

Here again, catalogued under the 'early United States Mint issues' is a small series of coins, very important to the American collector, but so rare that values are not ascribed to them in

Yeoman's catalogue. They bring the United States numismatic story to the year 1793, when the cataloguer begins to list the 'United States regular issues'.

These consist, or have consisted of the following denominations:

Copper Half Cents, 1793–1857.
Copper Large Cents, 1793–1857.
Copper-nickel Flying Eagle Cents, 1856–8.
Copper-nickel Indian Head Cents, 1859–64.
Bronze Small Indian Head Cents, 1864–1909.
Bronze Small Lincoln Head Cents, 1909 to date.
Bronze Two Cent Pieces, 1864–73.
Nickel Three Cent Pieces, 1865–89.
Nickel Five Cent Pieces, 1866 to date.
Silver Three Cent Pieces, 1851–73.
Silver Half Dimes, 1794–1873.
Silver Dimes, 1796 to date.
Silver Twenty Cent Pieces, 1875–8.
Silver Quarter Dollars, 1796 to date.
Silver Half Dollars, 1794 to date.
Silver Dollars, 1794–1935.
Gold Dollars, 1849–89.
Gold Quarter Eagles ($2½), 1796–1929.
Gold Three Dollar Pieces, 1854–89.
Gold Half Eagles ($5), 1795–1929.
Gold Eagles ($10), 1795–1933.
Gold Double Eagles ($20), 1849–1933.

To this list is added a long and interesting series of commemorative pieces, in various metals including gold, and a series of private or territorial gold coins.

Just as coins struck at the Royal Mint carry no mint mark, so those struck at Philadelphia, with certain exceptions, carry no distinguishing mark. In the exceptional cases the letter 'P' is used. Official mints in the United States are or were located at the following places:

Philadelphia, Pennsylvania, mint mark P
Charlotte, North Carolina, mint mark C

Carson City, Nevada, mint mark CC
Dahlonega, Georgia, mint mark D
Denver, Colorado, mint mark D
New Orleans, Louisiana, mint mark O
San Francisco, California, mint mark S

The two mint marks 'D' do not overlap in use, since Dahlonega used the mark, on gold coins only, from 1838 to 1861 and Denver on coins from 1906 to date.

It will be seen that with all this numismatic material at his disposal, the American collector has a nice compact series on which to focus his interests. It is a series predictable in the majority of cases as to size and shape, and is therefore easily housed. It can be catalogued in one pocket-size volume, which the keen collector can carry with him in his search for specimens. He frequently marks off in this book the various specimens he acquires.

To the American collector such coins as the English series must seem to straggle backwards into incomprehensible time, to be a mass of shapes, sizes and denominations, and to call for more effort in collecting than is compatible with a hobby. But, as stated earlier in this chapter, there is an increasing number of collectors in America who are turning to the more complex issues of the old world, and to the classical series of coins. It is seen that they provide a wider adventure in collecting. Books and catalogues in the American style are appearing, to assist this type of collecting.

Enough should have been said to show that the American collector is an unwearying enthusiast for his series, one full of many-sided interests, and complete within itself. Behind much of the collecting of United States and Canadian coins by the American collector lies a more direct appreciation of the investment value of the collection than is apparent in the average European collector. The American collector may strike it rich with some unknown and uncatalogued variety. The search for these goes on relentlessly. In any case the whole collection can be cashed in at any time if monetary resources should be needed. Many United States dealers will make cash advances based on the catalogue value of a collection.

Since any form of collecting is fundamentally to increase knowledge and erudition, to invest capital, to form a relaxation and to sharpen the faculties, wherein lies the difference between the American collector of United States coins, intensely preoccupied with apparent trivialities, and the collector of Anglo-Saxon pennies or Roman silver? Only in that the latter is often able to unearth important points of unknown numismatic history, while the former is preventing such points of history from becoming unknown.

We have tried in these pages to give some guidance as to how coins are collected. It matters not what coins one collects, the same basic feelings underlie the activities of every numismatist. Numismatics is a liberal science and study, one from which the numismatist reaps much of interest and value, not the least through friendship with others of his discipline.

Appendix I

THE RULERS OF ENGLAND AND THE COINS THEY ISSUED

From the time of Egbert (A.D. 802–839) the West Saxon kings extended their authority over most of the Southern English, and Edward the Elder and his successors exercised a varying amount of control over the Scandinavian kingdoms of the north. From 954 the control is permanent, and the kings who follow Edred (946–955) can claim to rule all England. The first of these was Edwy.

EDWY, 955–959
(Also known as Edwig)

Silver: penny.

EDGAR, 959–975

Silver: penny, halfpenny.

EDWARD THE MARTYR, 975–979

Silver: penny.

ETHELRED, 979–1016
(Also known as Æthelred II)

Silver: penny.

(*Note*: During this reign Swegn Forkbeard, King of Denmark, ruled from the autumn of 1013 till February 3, 1014, but was not crowned.)

EDMUND IRONSIDE, 1016

(Reigned from April till November 30; in Wessex only from the summer.)

CNUT, 1016–35

Silver: penny.

HAROLD I, 1035–40
(Also known as Harold Harefoot)

Silver: penny.

HARTHACNUT, 1040–42

Silver: penny.

EDWARD THE CONFESSOR, 1042–66

Silver: penny.

HAROLD II, 1066

Silver: penny.

EDGAR ETHLING, 1066

(Reigned only from October till December and was not crowned.)

WILLIAM I, 1066–87

Silver: penny.

WILLIAM II, 1087–1100

Silver: penny.

HENRY I, 1100–35

Silver: penny.

STEPHEN, 1135–54

Silver: penny.

(*Note*: During this reign irregular issues of coins were made by Eustace Fitzjohn, Robert de Stuteville, Henry of Blois, Bishop of Winchester, the Empress Matilda, Henry of Anjou, Robert of Gloucester, William of Gloucester, Brian Fitzcount or Baldwin de Redvers, and Patrick, Earl of Salisbury.)

HENRY II, 1154–89

Silver: penny.

RICHARD I, 1189–99

Silver: penny.

JOHN, 1199–1216

Silver: penny.

HENRY III, 1216–72

Silver: penny.

EDWARD I, 1272–1307

Silver: groat, penny, halfpenny, farthing.

EDWARD II, 1307–27

Silver: penny, halfpenny, farthing.

EDWARD III, 1327–77

Gold: florin, leopard or half-florin, helm or quarter-florin, noble, half-noble, quarter-noble.
Silver: groat, half-groat, penny, halfpenny, farthing.

RICHARD II, 1377–99

Gold: noble, half-noble, quarter-noble.
Silver: groat, half-groat, penny, halfpenny, farthing.

HENRY IV, 1399–1413

Gold: noble, half-noble, quarter-noble.
Silver: groat, half-groat, penny, halfpenny, farthing.

HENRY V, 1413–22

Gold: noble, half-noble, quarter-noble.
Silver: groat, half-groat, penny, halfpenny, farthing.

HENRY VI, 1422–61; restored 1470–71

Gold: noble, half-noble, quarter-noble, angel, half-angel.
Silver: groat, half-groat, penny, halfpenny, farthing.

EDWARD IV, 1461–83

(Divided into two reigns, 1461–70 and 1471–83)

Gold: noble, ryal or rose noble, half-ryal, quarter-ryal, angel, half-angel.
Silver: groat, half-groat, penny, halfpenny.

EDWARD V, 1483

Gold: angel, half-angel.
Silver: groat, penny, halfpenny. (A doubtful half-groat exists.)

RICHARD III, 1483–85

Gold: angel, half-angel.
Silver: groat, half-groat, penny, halfpenny.

HENRY VII, 1485–1509

Gold: sovereign, ryal or noble, angel, half-angel.
Silver: testoon or shilling, groat, half-groat, penny, halfpenny, farthing.

HENRY VIII, 1509–47

Gold: double sovereign, sovereign, half-sovereign, crown, half-crown, ryal or rose noble, angel, half-angel, quarter-angel, george noble, half-george noble.

Silver: testoon or shilling, groat, half-groat, penny, halfpenny, farthing.

EDWARD VI, 1547–53

Gold: triple sovereign, double sovereign, sovereign, half-sovereign, crown, half-crown, angel, half-angel.

Silver: crown, half-crown, shilling, sixpence, groat, threepence, half-groat, penny, halfpenny, farthing.

JANE, 1553 (uncrowned)

MARY, 1553–54

Gold: sovereign, ryal, angel, half-angel.

Silver: groat, half-groat, penny.

PHILIP AND MARY, 1554–58

Gold: angel, half-angel.

Silver: half-crown, shilling, sixpence, groat, half-groat, penny.

ELIZABETH I, 1558–1603

Gold: sovereign, ryal, half-sovereign, crown, half-crown, angel, half-angel, quarter-angel.

Silver: crown, half-crown, shilling, sixpence, groat, threepence, half-groat, three-halfpence, penny, three-farthings, half-penny.

JAMES I, 1603–25

Gold: sovereign or unit, half-sovereign or double crown, crown or Britain crown, half-crown, thistle crown, angel, half-angel, rose ryal or thirty-shilling piece, spur ryal or fifteen-shilling piece, laurel, half-laurel, quarter-laurel.

Silver: crown, half-crown, shilling, sixpence, half-groat, penny, halfpenny.

Copper: farthing.

CHARLES I, 1625–49

Gold: triple unit or three-pound piece, unit or twenty shillings, double crown or ten shillings, crown or five shillings, angel.

Silver: pound or twenty shillings, half-pound or ten shillings, crown, half-crown, shilling, sixpence, groat, half-groat, penny, halfpenny.

Copper: farthing.

COMMONWEALTH, 1649–60

Gold: twenty shillings or broad, ten shillings or half-broad, five shillings.
Silver: crown, half-crown, shilling, sixpence, half-groat, penny, half-penny.

OLIVER CROMWELL, 1653–58

Gold: fifty shillings, broad or twenty shillings, half-broad or ten shillings.
Silver: crown, half-crown, shilling, sixpence.
Copper: farthing.
(*Note*: These coins did not officially circulate and are usually regarded as patterns.)

CHARLES II, 1660–85

Gold: broad or twenty shillings, half-broad or ten shillings, crown or five shillings. Milled coins: five guineas, two guineas, guinea, half-guinea.
Silver: half-crown, shilling, sixpence, groat, threepence, half-groat, penny. Milled coins: crown, half-crown, shilling, sixpence, groat, threepence, half-groat, penny.
Copper: halfpenny, farthing.
Tin: farthing.

JAMES II, 1685–88

Gold: five guineas, two guineas, guinea, half-guinea.
Silver: crown, half-crown, shilling, sixpence, groat, threepence, half-groat, penny.
Tin: halfpenny, farthing.
Interregnum, 1688–89 (December to February).

WILLIAM AND MARY, 1689–94

Gold: five guineas, two guineas, guinea, half-guinea.
Silver: crown, half-crown, shilling, sixpence, groat, threepence, half-groat, penny.
Copper and tin: halfpenny, farthing.

WILLIAM III, 1694–1702

Gold: five guineas, two guineas, guinea, half-guinea.
Silver: crown, half-crown, shilling, sixpence, groat, threepence, half-groat, penny.
Copper: halfpenny, farthing.

ANNE, 1702–14

Gold: five guineas, two guineas, guinea, half-guinea.
Silver: crown, half-crown, sixpence, groat, threepence, half-groat, penny.
Copper: halfpenny, farthing (patterns only).

GEORGE I, 1714–27

Gold: five guineas, two guineas, guinea, half-guinea, quarter-guinea.
Silver: crown, half-crown, shilling, sixpence, groat, threepence, half-groat, penny.
Copper: halfpenny, farthing.

GEORGE II, 1727–60

Gold: five guineas, two guineas, guinea, half-guinea.
Silver: crown, half-crown, shilling, sixpence, groat, threepence, half-groat, penny.
Copper: halfpenny, farthing.

GEORGE III, 1760–1820

Gold: guinea, half-guinea, quarter-guinea, third-guinea or seven shillings, sovereign, half-sovereign.
Silver: crown, half-crown, shilling, sixpence, groat, threepence, half-groat, penny. Countermarked eight reales and Bank of England dollars.
Copper: twopence, penny, halfpenny, farthing.

GEORGE IV, 1820–30

Gold: double sovereign, sovereign, half-sovereign.
Silver: crown, half-crown, shilling, sixpence, groat, threepence, half-groat, penny.
Copper: penny, halfpenny, farthing.

WILLIAM IV, 1830–37

Gold: sovereign, half-sovereign.
Silver: half-crown, shilling, sixpence, groat, Maundy groat, threepence, half-groat, penny.
Copper: penny, halfpenny, farthing.

VICTORIA, 1837–1901

Gold: five pounds, two pounds, sovereign, half-sovereign.
Silver: crown, double florin or four shillings, half-crown, florin or two shillings, shilling, sixpence, groat, threepence,

Maundy groat, Maundy threepence, Maundy half-groat, Maundy penny.

Copper and bronze: penny, halfpenny, farthing.

EDWARD VII, 1901–10

Gold: five pounds, two pounds, sovereign, half-sovereign.

Silver: crown, half-crown, florin, shilling, sixpence, Maundy groat, threepence, Maundy half-groat, Maundy penny.

Bronze: penny, halfpenny, farthing.

GEORGE V, 1910–36

Gold: five pounds, two pounds (proofs only), sovereign, half-sovereign.

Silver: crown, half-crown, florin, shilling, sixpence, threepence, Maundy groat, Maundy threepence, Maundy half-groat, Maundy penny.

Bronze: penny, halfpenny, farthing.

EDWARD VIII, 1936 (uncrowned)

The coins struck for circulation during this reign had the head of George V. A very small number of twelve-sided threepence pieces with the head of Edward VIII passed from the Mint on test. A complete set of proofs, from five pounds to bronze penny, exists.

GEORGE VI, 1936–52

Gold: five pounds, two pounds, sovereign, half-sovereign (proofs only).

Silver: crown, half-crown, florin, shilling (English), shilling (Scottish), sixpence, threepence, Maundy groat, threepence, half-groat, penny.

Cupro-nickel: crown, half-crown, florin, shilling (English), shilling (Scottish), sixpence.

Nickel-bronze: threepence.

Bronze: penny, halfpenny, farthing.

ELIZABETH II, 1952

Gold: Sovereign.

Silver: Maundy groat, threepence, half-groat, penny.

Cupro-nickel: crown, half-crown, florin, shilling (English), shilling (Scottish), sixpence.

Nickel-bronze: threepence.

Bronze: penny, halfpenny, farthing.

Appendix II
THE RULERS OF SCOTLAND AND THE COINS THEY ISSUED

Before the beginning of the twelfth century the currency in Scotland was mainly of Anglo-Saxon and English pennies and Northumbrian stycas. The earliest coins which can definitely be assigned to any Scottish ruler are the pennies of David I. Even after his accession there were more English than Scottish coins in circulation in Scotland, and this continued till the reigns of Edward I, II and III. By that time the ratio of English over Scottish coins was about thirty to one.

DAVID I, 1124–53

Silver: penny.

HENRY, EARL OF HUNTINGDON AND NORTHUMBERLAND, 1139–52

Silver: penny.

MALCOLM IV, 1153–65

Silver: penny.

WILLIAM THE LION, 1165–1214

Silver: penny.

ALEXANDER II, 1214–49

Silver: penny.

ALEXANDER III, 1249–85

Silver: penny, halfpenny and farthing.

JOHN BALIOL, 1292–96

Silver: penny and halfpenny.

ROBERT BRUCE, 1306–29

Silver: penny, halfpenny and farthing.

DAVID II, 1329–71

Gold: noble.
Silver: groat, half-groat penny, halfpenny, farthing.

ROBERT II, 1371–90

Silver: groat, half-groat, penny, halfpenny.

ROBERT III, 1390–1406

Gold: St. Andrew or lion, demi-lion or demy.
Silver: groat, half-groat, penny, halfpenny.

JAMES I, 1406–37

Gold: demy and half-demy.
Silver: groat.
Billon: penny.

JAMES II, 1437–60

Gold: demy, lion, half-lion.
Silver: groat, half-groat, penny.
Billon: penny.

JAMES III, 1460–88

Gold: rider, half-rider, quarter-rider, unicorn, half-unicorn.
Silver: groat, half-groat, penny.
Billon: penny, plack, half-plack.
Copper: farthing.

JAMES IV, 1488–1514

Gold: lion, half-lion, unicorn, half-unicorn.
Silver: groat, half-groat, penny.
Billon: plack, penny.

JAMES V, 1514–42

Gold: unicorn, half-unicorn, ecu or crown, ducat or bonnet-piece, two-thirds, bonnet-piece, one-third bonnet-piece.
Silver: groat, half-groat.
Billon: plack, bawbee, half-bawbee.

MARY, 1542–67

Gold: ecu, twenty shillings, lion, half-lion, ryal, half-ryal, ducat, crown.
Silver: testoon, half-testoon, ryal, two-thirds ryal, one-third ryal.
Billon: bawbee, half-bawbee, penny, plack, twelve-penny groat or *nonsunt*, lion or hardhead.

JAMES VI, 1567–1625

Period I. Before Accession to the English Throne.

Gold: twenty-pound piece, ducat or four-pound piece, lion noble, two-thirds lion noble, one-third lion noble, thistle noble, hat-piece, rider, half-rider, sword and sceptre-piece, half-sword and sceptre-piece.

Silver: ryal or thirty-shilling piece, two-thirds ryal or twenty-shilling piece, one-third ryal or ten-shilling piece, noble or half-merk, half-noble or quarter-merk, double merk or thistle dollar, merk or half-thistle dollar, sixteen-shilling piece, eight-shilling piece, four-shilling piece, two-shilling piece, forty-shilling piece, thirty-shilling piece, twenty-shilling piece, ten-shilling piece, balance half-merk, balance quarter-merk, ten-shilling piece, five-shilling piece, thirty-penny piece, twelve-penny piece, thistle merk, half-thistle merk, quarter-thistle merk, eighth-thistle merk.

Billon: plack, half-plack, hardhead or lion, half-hardhead, saltire plack.

Copper: twopence, penny.

Period II (1603–25). After Accession to the English Throne.

Gold: unit or sceptre, double crown, Britain crown, half-crown, thistle crown.

Silver: sixty shillings, thirty shillings, twelve shillings, six shillings, two shillings, shilling, half-shilling.

Copper: turner or twopence, half-turner or penny.

CHARLES I, 1625–49

Gold: unit or sceptre, half-unit or double crown, quarter-unit or Britain crown, eighth-unit or half-crown.

Silver: three-pound piece or crown, sixty shillings, thirty shillings, twelve shillings, six shillings, three shillings, two shillings, shilling, half-shilling, half-merk, forty-penny piece, twenty penny piece.

Copper: turner or twopence, half-turner or penny.

CHARLES II, 1660–85

Silver: four-merk piece, two-merk piece, merk, half-merk, dollar, half-dollar, quarter-dollar, eighth-dollar, sixteenth-dollar.

Copper: turner, bawbee or sixpence, bodle or twopence.

JAMES VII, 1685–88

Silver: sixty-shilling piece, forty-shilling piece, ten-shilling piece.

WILLIAM AND MARY, 1689–94

Silver: sixty-shilling piece, forty-shilling piece, twenty-shilling piece, ten-shilling piece, five-shilling piece.

Copper: bawbee, bodle.

WILLIAM II (III OF ENGLAND), 1694–1702

Gold: pistole, half-pistole.
Silver: sixty-shilling piece, forty-shilling piece, twenty-shilling piece, ten-shilling piece, five-shilling piece.
Copper: bawbee, bodle.

ANNE, 1702–14

Silver: ten-shilling piece, five-shilling piece, crown, half-crown, shilling, sixpence.

(*Note*: This is the last coinage struck in Scotland. The Scottish shilling, struck in 1937 and from then onwards, was introduced as a compliment to Elizabeth, Queen Consort of George VI, and was struck in London. It is not a true Scottish coin.)

JAMES VIII, 1716

A crown-piece was prepared in Paris for Prince James, the Old Pretender, but no contemporary specimens were struck.

The coinage of Scotland is now assimilated with that of England.

APPENDIX III
THE RULERS OF IRELAND AND THE COINS THEY ISSUED

THE Irish series starts with Hiberno-Danish issues. The earliest coins struck in Ireland are either of late tenth or early eleventh century. A series of pennies bear the name of Æthelred II of Wessex, and these were struck in Dublin. He could not himself have struck these Irish coins, and they are therefore considered as imitations, struck by native rulers. The first English coins struck in Ireland were issued by John, son of Henry II, in his title of Lord of Ireland. For purposes of completeness the coins in this Appendix start with the imitations of Æthelred II, since they at least served the purpose of money.

ÆTHELRED II, 979–1016

Silver: penny.

These are followed by the pennies struck in imitation of the money of Sihtric III, who was a contemporary of Æthelred II.

SIHTRIC III, 989–1029

Silver: penny. Hiberno-English issues.

JOHN, AS LORD OF IRELAND, 1177–99

Silver: halfpenny, farthing.

JOHN, AS KING, 1199–1216

Silver: penny, halfpenny, farthing.

HENRY III, 1216–72

Silver: penny, halfpenny.

EDWARD I, II, AND III, 1272–1377

Silver: penny, halfpenny, farthing.

RICHARD II AND HENRY IV AND V, 1377–1422

There are no coins which can be attributed with certainty to these kings.

HENRY VI, 1422–61 AND 1470–71

Silver: groat, penny.
Copper: half-farthing or Patrick.

EDWARD IV, 1461–83

Silver: double groat, groat, half-groat, penny, halfpenny, farthing.
Copper: farthing, half-farthing.

EDWARD V, 1483

No coins were with certainty attributed to this ruler, who only reigned from April to June 1483. In 1941 the late Mr. Carlyon-Britton established that groats and pennies were struck at both the Dublin and Drogheda mints which are attributable to this short reign. The same authority also established that certain of these coins were later altered to serve the next reign.

RICHARD III, 1483–85

Silver: groat, penny.

HENRY VII, 1485–1509

Silver: groat, half-groat, penny.

In May 1487 Lambert Simnel was crowned in Dublin as Edward VI. His coinage consisted of groats. A penny, believed to be a unique specimen, was also struck for this reign. The coins were minted at Trim.

In June of the same year Simnel and his followers were defeated in battle by the forces of Henry VII.

HENRY VIII, 1509–47

Silver: groat, half-groat.

EDWARD VI, 1547–53

Silver: shilling, groat, half-groat, penny, halfpenny.

MARY, 1553–54

Silver: shilling, groat, half-groat, penny.

PHILIP AND MARY, 1554–58

Silver: shilling, groat.

ELIZABETH I, 1558–1603

Silver: shilling, sixpence, groat, threepence.
Copper: penny, halfpenny.

JAMES I, 1603–25

Silver: shilling, sixpence.
Copper: farthing.

CHARLES I, 1625–49

Copper: farthing.

Money of necessity.

Inchiquin money, Gold: pistole (only about two specimens known).
Silver: crown, half-crown, shilling, ninepence, groat.
Dublin money. Silver: crown, half-crown.
Kilkenny money. Copper: halfpenny.
'Blacksmith's' money. Silver: half-crown.
Ormonde money. Silver: crown, half-crown, shilling, sixpence, fourpence, threepence, twopence.
Rebel money. Silver: crown, half-crown.
Cork money. Silver: shilling. sixpence.
Copper: penny (?).

Other copper coins struck at this period emanate from Bandon, Kinsale and Youghal.

COMMONWEALTH, 1649–60

No official money issued for special circulation in Ireland. Local copper penny, halfpenny and farthing tokens appeared. They are normally classified under seventeenth-century tokens.

CHARLES II, 1649–85

Silver: crown, half-crown.
Copper: halfpenny, farthing.

JAMES II, 1685–88

Copper: halfpenny.
Gun metal: crown, half-crown, shilling, sixpence.
White metal: groat.
Pewter: crown, penny, halfpenny.
Brass: halfpenny.

WILLIAM AND MARY, 1689–94

Copper: halfpenny.

WILLIAM III, 1694–1702

Copper: halfpenny.

ANNE, 1702–14

No money struck for Ireland in this reign.

GEORGE I, 1714–27

Copper: halfpenny, farthing.

GEORGE II, 1727–60

Copper: halfpenny, farthing.

GEORGE III, 1760–1820

Silver: six-shilling, thirty-pence, ten-pence, five-pence (Bank of Ireland tokens).
Copper: penny, halfpenny, farthing.

GEORGE IV, 1820–30

Copper: penny, halfpenny.
1823–1928: coinage assimilated to that of Great Britain.

REPUBLIC OF IRELAND, 1928

Silver: half-crown, shilling, sixpence.
Nickel: threepence.
Bronze: penny, halfpenny, farthing.

Appendix IV
AN ALPHABETICAL CHART OF ENGLISH MINT MARKS

MINT MARK	SYMBOL	OCCURS IN REIGNS OF
Acorn		Henry VIII, Elizabeth I
Arrow		Henry VIII, Edward VI
A		Elizabeth I
Annulet		Edward IV
Annulet and pellet		Edward IV, Henry VIII
Anchor		Henry VII, Elizabeth I, Charles I, Commonwealth
Anchor and B		Charles I
Boar's head		Edward V, Richard III
Boar's head		Richard III
Boar's head		Charles I
Bow		Edward VI
Br		Charles I
Bell		Elizabeth I, James I, Charles I
Book		James I, Charles I
Cross		Edward III
Cross: broken		Edward III
Cross		Edward III
Cross potent		Edward III
Cross pattée		Edward III, Richard II, Henry IV, Henry V, Henry VI, Edward IV, Charles I
Cross: plain		Henry VI, Edward IV, Henry VIII, Elizabeth I, James I
Cross potence		Henry VI, Henry VIII
Cross fleurée		Henry VI, Edward IV
Cross calvery		Charles I
Cross: long fitchée		Edward IV, Henry VII, Henry VIII

MINT MARK	SYMBOL	OCCURS IN REIGNS OF
Cross: short fitchée		Henry VI, Edward IV
Cross: Restoration		Henry VI
Cross: Latin		Elizabeth I
Cross: voided		Henry VI, Henry VIII
Cross: Saltire		James I
Cross and pellets		Edward IV
Cross: pierced		Henry V, Henry VI, Edward IV
Cross: pierced and pellets	THE PEL MAY VARY	Edward IV
Cross: pellet in central piercing		Edward IV
Cross crosslet		Henry VII, Philip and Mary
Cinquefoil		James I
Cinquefoil		Edward IV, Henry VII
Catherine Wheel		Henry VIII
Castle		Henry VIII
Castle		Elizabeth I, James I, Charles I
Castle and H		Henry VIII
Crescent		Elizabeth I, James I
Crescent		Henry VIII
Coronet		Edward III, Henry IV, Edward IV, Philip and Mary, Charles I
Crown		Charles I
Crozier		Edward III, Henry VII
Dragon		Henry VII
Eglantine		Elizabeth I
Ermine		Elizabeth I
Escallop		Henry VII, Henry VIII, Edward VI
Escallop		Elizabeth I, James I
Eye		Charles I
Flower and B	B	Charles I
Gerb	OR	Charles I
Grapes		James I, Charles I
Greyhound's head		Henry VII

MINT MARK	SYMBOL	OCCURS IN REIGNS OF
Grapple		Edward VI
Hand		Elizabeth I
Harp		Charles I
Heart		Charles I
Helmet		Charles I
Key	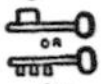	Henry VIII, Elizabeth I, James I
Lis on rose		Henry VII
Lis on rose and sun		Henry VII
Lis and rose dimidiate		Henry VII
Lis issuing from rose		Henry VII
Leopard's head		Henry VII, Charles I
Lion		Edward VI, Elizabeth I, Charles I
Lion rampant		Charles I
Lis		Henry VI, Edward IV, Henry VII, Henry VIII, Edward VI, Philip and Mary, Elizabeth I, James I, Charles I
Lis		Henry VIII, Elizabeth I
Mullet		Henry V, James I, Charles I
Mullet pierced		Edward VI, Elizabeth I
Martlet		Henry VII, Henry VIII, Edward VI, Elizabeth I
Negro's head		Charles I
Ostrich head		Edward VI
Pansy		Henry VII, Henry VIII
Pheon		Henry VII, Henry VIII, Edward VI, Elizabeth I
Pomegranate		Henry VIII
P in brackets	(P)	Charles I
Pall	Y	Edward IV
Pear		Charles I
Plume		Charles I
Plume: Aberystwyth		Charles I
Plume: Shrewsbury		Charles I

MINT MARK	SYMBOL	OCCURS IN REIGNS OF
Plume: Oxford		Charles I
Portcullis		Elizabeth I, Charles I
Portcullis crowned		Henry VIII
Rose		Henry VI, Edward IV, Henry VII, Henry VIII, Edward VI, Elizabeth I, James I
Rose		Charles I
R in brackets	(R)	Charles I
Star, rayout		Henry VIII
Star		Henry VIII, Elizabeth I, Charles I
Spur rowel		James I
Sun		Edward IV
Sun		James I, Charles I, Commonwealth
Sun halved		Edward IV, Edward V, Richard III
Sun halved		Richard III, Henry VII
Sceptre		Charles I
Sunburst		Henry VIII
Swan		Edward VI
Sword		Elizabeth I
Six (6)	6	Edward VI
Trefoil		Henry VI, Edward IV, Henry VIII, Edward VI
Trefoil slipped		Henry VI, James I
Trefoil slipped		James I
T	T	Edward VI
T C	TC	Edward VI
Triangle	△	Charles I
Triangle in circle		Charles I
Tun		Henry VII, Edward VI, Elizabeth I, James I, Charles I
Thistle		James I
W.S.	WS	Henry VIII, Edward VI
Woolpack		Elizabeth I
Y	 y y	Edward VI

(By courtesy Spink & Son Ltd.)

APPENDIX V

THE NAMES OF THE ROMAN EMPERORS, 27 B.C. TO A.D. 423

(*Note: Only the more important usurpers are included*)

Augustus, 27 B.C.–A.D. 14
Tiberius, A.D. 14–37
Gaius (Caligula) 37–41
Claudius, 41–54
Nero, 54–68
Galba, A.D. 68–69
Otho, 69
Vitellius, 69
Vespasian, 69–79
Titus, 79–81
Domitian, 81–96
Nerva, 96–98
Trajan, 98–117
Hadrian, 117–138
Antoninus Pius, 138–161
Marcus Aurelius, 161–180
Lucius Verus, 161–169
Commodus, 180–192
Pertinax, 193
Didius Julianus, 193
Pescennius Niger, 193–194
Septimius Severus, 193–211
Clodius Albinus, 193–197
Caracalla, 211–217
Geta, 211–212
Macrinus, 217–218
Elagabalus, 218–222
Severus Alexander, 222–235
Maximinus I, 235–238
Gordian I, Gordian II, } 238 (Joint Emperors)
Balbinus, Pupienus, } 238 (Joint Emperors)
Gordian III, 238–244
Philip I, 244–249; Philip II, 247–249 } Joint Emperors
Trajan Decius, 249–251
Trebonianus Gallus, 251–253
Æmilian, 253
Valerian, 253–259; Gallienus, 253–268 } Joint Emperors
Postumus, 258–268; Victorinus, 265–268; Marius, 268; Tetricus, 268–273 } Usurpers in Gaul
Claudius Gothicus, 268–270
Quintillus, 270
Aurelian, 270–275
Tacitus, 275–276
Florian, 276
Probus, 276–282
Carus, 282–283
Carinus and Numerian, 282/3 284/5
Diocletian, 285–305; Maximian 286–305 } Joint Emperors
Carausius, 286–293; Allectus, 293–296 } Usurpers of Britain
Constantius I, 305–306
Galerius Maximianus, 305–310
Severus, 306–307
Maxentius, 306–312
Maximinus II, 308–314
Licinius, 308–324

Constantine I, 306–337
Constantine II, 337–340
Constantius II, 337–361
Constans, 337–350
Magnentius, 350–353
Julian 361–363
Jovian, 363–364
Valentinian I, 364–375
Valens, 364–378
Gratian, 367–383
Valentinian II, 375–392
Theodosius, 378–395
Maximus, 383–388 (usurper in Britain)
Arcadius, 395–408 (Eastern Empire)
Honorius, 395–423 (Western Empire)

Appendix VI
BIBLIOGRAPHY: USEFUL WORKS FOR FURTHER READING

ON GREEK COINS

HEAD, B. V. *A Guide to the Principal Coins of the Greeks.* 1959.
HEAD, B. V. *Historia Numorum, a manual of Greek Numismatics.* 1911, reprinted 1963.
NEWELL, E. T. *Royal Greek Portrait Coins.* 1937, reprinted 1963.
SEABY, H. A. *Greek Coins & Their Values.* 1966
SELTMAN, C. T. *Greek Coins.* 1960.
SELTMAN, C. T. *Masterpieces of Greek Coinage.* 1949.

ON ROMAN AND BYZANTINE COINS

GOODACRE, H. *A Handbook of the Coinage of the Byzantine Empire.* 1964.
HILL, SIR GEORGE. *Becker, the Counterfeiter.* 1965 edition.
KENT, J. P. C., CARSON, R. A. G. and HILL, P. V. *Late Roman Bronze Coinage.* 1960.
KLAWANS, Z. H. *Reading and Dating Roman Imperial Coins.* 1959.
MATTINGLY, H. *Roman Coins, from the earliest times to the fall of the Western Empire.* 1962 edition.
SEAR, D. R. *Roman Coins and their values.* 1964.
SYDENHAM, E. A. *The Coinage of the Roman Republic.* 1952. Reprinting, with revisions.

ON COINS IN GENERAL

ALLEN, J. J. CULLIMORE. *The History of the British Sovereign.* 1965
BRESSETT, K. E. *A Guide Book of English Coins.* 1966–1967 edition.
BRETON, P. N. *Popular Illustrated Guide to Canadian Coins, Medals (etc.).* Reprint.
BROOKE, G. C. *English Coins.* 1962 edition.
CARSON, R. A. G. *Coins, ancient, mediaeval and modern.* 1962.
CHARLTON, *J. E. Standard Catalogue of Canadian Coins, Tokens and Paper Money.* 1967 edition.
CLAIN-STEPHANELLI, E. E. *Russian Gold Coins.* 1962.
CRAIG, W. D. *Coins of the World, 1750–1850.* 1966. One of the volumes referred to (p. 9) as a modest start on a catalogue of the coins of the whole world.
CLARKE, R. L. *Catalog of the Coins of British Oceania.* 1964.
COOLE, A. B. *Coins in China's History.* 1963.

CROGHAN, J. R. *Canadian Cent Varieties*. 1963.

DOLLEY, R. H. M. *Anglo-Saxon Pennies*. 1964.

DOLLEY, R. H. M. *The Norman Conquest and the English Coinage*. 1966.

DUVEEN, SIR G. AND STRIDE H. G. *The History of the Gold Sovereign*. 1962.

FRIEDBERG, R. *Gold Coins of the World, complete from 600 A.D. to the present*. Second edition. One of the volumes referred to in the Preface to the third edition as a modest start on a catalogue of the coins of the whole world.

FRIEDBERG, R. *Coins of the British World, complete from 500 A.D. to the present*.

JUDD, J. H. *United States Pattern, Experimental and Trial Pieces*. 1962.

KADMAN, L. *Israel's Money*. 1963.

KAPLAN, A. *The Coins of South Africa*. 1962.

LINECAR, H. W. A. (Editor). *The Milled Coinage of England, 1662–1946*.

LINECAR, H. W. A. *British Commonwealth Coinage*. 1959.

LINECAR, H. W. A. *The Crown Pieces of Great Britain and the British Commonwealth*. 1962.

LINECAR, H. W. A. *Beginner's Guide to Coin Collecting*. 1966.

LINECAR, H. W. A. AND STONE, A. G. *A Catalogue of Pattern and Proof Crown Size Coins of Britain and the Commonwealth*. In active preparation.

LE MAY. *The Coinage of Siam*. 1961.

MACK, R. P. *The Coinage of Ancient Britain*. Second edition, 1964.

METCALF, DR. D. M. *The Coinage of South Germany in the Thirteenth Century*. 1961.

MISHLER, C. *United States and Canadian Commemorative Medals and Tokens*. 1966 edition.

NORTH, J. J. *English Hammered Coinage*. Two volumes.

NEWCOMB, H. R. *United States Copper Cents, 1816–1857*.

SPINK & SON. *Catalogue of Papal Medals*. 1962 reprint of the original Lincoln catalogue.

PARSONS, H. A. *The Colonial Coinages of British Africa, with the adjacent islands*. 1950.

PRIDMORE, CAPTAIN F. *The Coins of the British Commonwealth of Nations to the end of the reign of George VI*.

Part 1. *European Territories*.

Part 2. *Asian Territories, excluding India*.

Part 3. *The West Indies*.

Part 4. *India*, in active preparation.

PURVEY, F. *Collecting Coins*. 1962.

QUIGGIN, A. H. *A Survey of Primitive Money*. 1964.

RUDY, W. A. *Commemorative Coins of the United States*.

SCHOLTEN, C. *The Coins of the Dutch Overseas Territories*. 1953.

SANDHAM, A. *Coins, Tokens and Medals of the Dominion of Canada.*
SEABY, B. A., Ltd. *Standard Catalogue of British Coins.* 1967 edition.
SEABY, B. A., LTD. *British Copper Coins and their values.* 1963.
SEABY, B. A., LTD. *British Coins, 1816-1965.*
SEVERIN, H. M. *Gold and Platinum Coinage of Imperial Russia, 1701–1911.*
SEVERIN, H. M. *The Silver Coinage of Imperial Russia.* 1965.
SHAW, E. M. *A History of Currency in South Africa.* 1956
SHAFER, N. *United States Territorial Coinage for the Philippine Islands.* 1961.
STEWART, B. H. I. H. *The Scottish Coinage.* Second edition in active preparation.
STRIDE, H. G. *The Royal Mint, an outline history.* 1960.
TAYLOR, H. C., SOMER JAMES, AND GERBINSKY, N. *The Guide Book of Canadian Coins, Currency & Tokens with, The Guide Book of Great Britain's Modern Coins.* Various editions.
TAXEY, D. *Counterfeit, Mis-struck and Unofficial U.S. Coins.*
THOMPSON, J. D. A. *Inventory of British Coin Hoards, 660–1500.* 1956.
WAYTE RAYMOND. *The Silver Dollars of North and South America.* Reprinted with revisions, 1964.
DAVENPORT, DR. J. Volume I. *European Crowns and Talers since 1800.* 1964.
Volume II. *European Crowns, 1700–1800.* 1965.
Volume III. *German Talers, 1700–1800.* 1965.
YEOMAN, R. S. *Catalog of Modern World Coins.* 6th edition. One of the volumes referred to (p. 9) as a modest start on a catalogue of the coins of the whole world.
YEOMAN, R. S. *A Guide Book of United States Coins.* 1967 edition.

Sylloge of Coins of the British Isles. This is a work of major importance and highly specialised. At the time of going to press it had reached some 9 volumes, dealing mainly with Ancient British and Anglo-Saxon Coins. In his Foreword to the first volume in the series (1958), Sir Frank Stenton wrote: 'The idea of a *Sylloge of the Coins of the British Isles* was originated by the British Numismatic Society. It has received the support of the British Academy, which has appointed a Committee to carry the project into effect. Each of these bodies has given financial assistance to the scheme.' Since that time the Committee's target of 'a volume a year' has been attained.

ON TOKEN COINAGES

Here there is an aching void. All the standard works are out of print, and most of them need considerable revision. It is possible to give only a few recent works which are available, in the hope that there may be more to come.

BELL, R. C. *Commercial Coins, 1787–1804.* 1963.
BELL, R. C. *Copper Commercial Coins, 1811-1819.*
MATHIAS, P. *English Trade Tokens.* 1962.
SEABY, H. A. AND BUSHELL, M. *British Copper Coins and their values.* 1965.
WETTON, J. L. *The Hampshire Seventeenth Century Traders' Tokens.* 1964.
WETTON, J. L. *The Isle of Wight Seventeenth Century Traders' Tokens.*

PERIODICALS

The Numismatic Chronicle. Published annually.
The British Numismatic Journal. Published annually.
Coins and Medals. Published monthly.
Coin Monthly. Published monthly.
The Numismatic Circular. A private publication issued by Spink & Son, Ltd. Eleven issues per year, on subscription.
The Coin & Medal Bulletin. A private publication issued by B. A. Seaby, Ltd. on subscription.
The Numismatic Gazette. A private publication, issued by Corbitt & Hunter, Ltd. on subscription.
Australian Numismatic Journal.
The Australian Coin Review.
Calcoin News.
Canadian Coin News.
The Canadian Numismatic Journal.
Coin Galleries Numismatic Review and Fixed Price List.
Coin World.
The Colonial Newsletter.
The Journal of the Token and Medal Society.
New Zealand Numismatic Journal.
Numismatic News.
The Numismatic Scrapbook Magazine.
The Numismatist.
The Whitman Numismatic Journal.
World Coins.

There are many other numismatic periodicals published throughout the world, and in Europe in particular. The American Numismatic Society's quarterly, *Numismatic Literature,* reviews them all, and is obtainable from the Society, located at Broadway between 155th and 156th Street, New York, N.Y. 10032, U.S.A.

Index

[*Bold figures refer to plate numbers*]

Printed in Great Britain by
Cox & Wyman Limited
London Fakenham and Reading